# The Ultimate Guide to Christian Singleness

# By Mark Ballenger

If you desire to glorify God through your singleness, this book is for you.

# Table of Contents

# Introduction

## Don't Worry, There Really Are Answers

Every Christian's life is unique. Each one of us goes through peaks and valleys which are different that someone else's peaks and valleys. While no two Christian lives are exactly the same, there is one season of life I can guarantee we all will experience: Christian singleness.

Nobody is born married. And while in some cultures arranged marriages can happen at a young age, even then there is a time of singleness before the marriage actually occurs. Most of us are given choices when it comes to marriage, which is obviously a good thing. But with choices comes much confusion. While each Christian's season of singleness will be different, there are also many commonalities that we all will experience in this stage of life.

Am I ever going to find the right person? Is God calling me to a life of singleness? Do I look good enough to attract a spouse I am attracted to? How will we meet? Should I try online dating since this whole process is taking longer than I thought it would? Is there anything I can do to speed up this process of finding a Christian spouse? Does God think I am discontent with him because I want a spouse? Is God not blessing my search because of my sin? If God is sovereign and he loves me, why isn't he blessing me with this amazing gift of marriage? What practical things should I do and not do to find a spouse?

Our list of questions stemming from singleness could go on forever. But perhaps what is even worse than all the unknowns during this season is the emotions that come along with all of these questions.

Let's get real with each other for just a minute. How do you feel when you see a friend of yours announce on social media that she is engaged? And then another friend, and another friend, and another friend, all while you remain single? How do you feel when you see the pictures of her ring? What emotions go on inside when you see your buddy standing there with a beautiful woman, a woman just like you hope to find one day? When you see the wedding day photos, what emotions rise in you? What goes on in your mind when the bride and groom embrace each other? What uncomfortable feelings bubble to the surface of your heart when you begin to wonder when it will finally be your turn to make that engagement announcement on social media?

Most Christian singles I've talked to and counseled have said moments like these hurt. Of course you are happy for your friends when they get married. It's not like we are saying our pain would be eased if others didn't find love either. But seeing someone else enjoy romance often awakens feelings in us that we have tried to push down. It's okay to admit that it feels like a jab every time someone else finds love when you still haven't. This is all part of the process. God is preparing you for your future.

I want to encourage you that there are answers found in God's word. The title of this book is "The Ultimate Guide to Christian Singleness." I wanted to add in parenthesis, "except for the Bible." Obviously the word of God is the best book to answer any question we have about singleness. God alone can provide the wisdom we need (James 1:5). But because this guidebook is rooted deeply in Scripture, I believe God can use it to really help you find the guidance you are looking for.

I got married at the age of twenty-two but my wife was twenty-seven, so I have a firsthand glimpse at getting married at the beginning or tail-end of the twenties. By the grace of God, I've also been blessed with the experience of being a pastor to older adults, young adults, and teens – and all of these groups of people needed relationship counseling, especially when it came to singleness.

I love counseling people on how to biblically approach relationships, which is why I went to seminary and got a master's degree in the field of pastoral counseling. All that to say, I am pumped to put all that I've learned into one easy-to-use, condensed, and practical manual for anyone looking to glorify God during their season of Christian singleness.

God uses everything for his glory. He has a purpose for you during your singleness, and it is your job to figure out what that is. And I want to help you. What is God trying to teach you right now? How is he preparing you for a healthy future marriage (or for a life of godly singleness if that's his will for you)? If we don't answer these questions, odds are will be underprepared for the seasons ahead and suffer the consequences.

## How to Use this Guidebook

In closing, here are a few pointers as you read through this guidebook. You certainly can read this book cover to cover. It's been formatted in a logical progression by laying a biblical foundation on singleness right at the beginning (Section 1). I then give you the knowledge needed to thrive during your season of singleness or through your life of celibacy (Section 2). Next we move into the practical nuts and bolts needed to prepare for your future (Section 3). Finally, this guide closes by diving into how you can be practical and put yourself in the best possible position to find the spouse God has for you (Section 4).

But you don't have to read this book cover to cover to benefit from it. It's also been designed like a survival manual, an encyclopedia, or a cookbook. You can just go to the table of contents, look at what topics you need to read, and start studying.

After each chapter there are some reflection questions. It's best if you can go through these with a friend who is also single, a small group Bible study of Christian singles, or perhaps even an older mentor who has walked these roads before. You can also just use these questions for personal reflection. Either way, I highly recommend you spend a few minutes answering these questions as they will really help the information sink in and prepare you to actually apply what you've been studying.

I don't know your story. I don't know the specifics of what God has in store for your future. But I do know God loves you and has an amazing life planned for you. Through every season, no matter what your relationship status is or isn't, God has good planned for you.

It definitely won't be an easy life. But if you walk closely with Jesus, I can promise you it will be a great life filled with fun, trials, loss, adventure, and glorifying God.

## Study Questions

1. Why are you reading his book? What are some specific questions you want to find answers to?

2. How would you describe your relationship past? Share some of the most important details with the group (or write them down for yourself). How have these experiences or lack of experiences affected you? (If you're having trouble answering this question, answer this: What is your first reaction/feeling when you hear the word "singleness?")

3. If you are in a group, list some specific hopes and expectations each group member has for this study and pray together. If you are doing this by yourself, write out a prayer to God, asking him to help you in the specific areas where you would like to grow.

# Section 1

# A Biblical Foundation of Christian Singleness

# Chapter 1

# What Does the Bible Say About Singleness?

What does the Bible say about singleness? Is Christian singleness a curse or a blessing?

The Bible answers questions like these indirectly and directly. What follows is a foundational understanding of what the Bible says about singleness.

## The Bible Says Singleness Can Be a Blessing

Everyone goes through a season of singleness. Some remain single for longer, but for all, even if it is just for a season, God wants us to know that singleness can be a blessing.

Paul explains throughout 1 Corinthians 7 that the great blessing to singleness is that it makes life easier in practical ways and thus allows us to be better equipped to focus on God and serve him in Christian ministry. He goes on, however, to qualify these statements by saying that those who are gifted differently than him (Paul was single) will be better equipped to serve God through marriage.

So the Bible says that singleness and marriage are both blessings from the Lord, "I wish that all were as I myself am [single]. But each has his own gift from God, one of one kind and one of another" (1 Corinthians 7:7). On the gift of singleness, Elizabeth Elliot said:

> "Having now spent more than forty-one years single, I have learned that it is indeed a gift. Not one I would

choose. Not one many [people] would choose. But we do not choose our gifts, remember? We are given them by a divine Giver who knows the end from the beginning, and wants above all else to give us the gift of Himself."[1]

Elizabeth Elliot lost her husband when he was martyred on the mission field. But God taught her that the great blessing to singleness, even an unwanted singleness, is that it can help you focus on God. Some of you may want to be single, but some of you may not. For all of us, however, our season of singleness can be a blessing if we use it to seek God.

## The Bible Says Singleness Can Be a Consequence for Sin

Notice I've been using the language "singleness can be a blessing." I've used the words "can be" because singleness isn't always a blessing. Sometimes it can be a consequence for sin.

When it comes to each individual, I have no clue which it is. I would never tell someone their singleness is a consequence of their sin because only God has that kind of sovereign knowledge of cause and effect. But theologically and hypothetically, singleness can be a consequence for sin sometimes.

I believe in most cases, singleness is just a natural part of God's plan for someone which he intends to use as a blessing in their life. But to assume that humans have no active role to play in their relationship status is just unbiblical.

Certainly God is in control, but the way that plays out in real life is not like a puppet show. Our choices and sins do have consequences, and sometimes this means God wanted to bless you with marriage but your sinfulness blocked his blessing.

For example, Proverbs 19:14 states, "House and wealth are inherited from fathers, but a prudent wife is from the LORD" and Proverbs 18:22 says, "He who finds a wife finds a good thing and obtains favor from the Lord." From these verses we can make the statement that a healthy Christian marriage is a gift from God.

We must also recognize that God often removes his favor when we rebel and don't repent. God's grace never runs out, but he will at times remove his favor to get our attention. Sometimes he won't bless someone when they are living in sin because to do so would only encourage their sinful behavior. God knows that sometimes, people won't repent unless they get hurt so bad they know their only chance is to run back to him (Luke 15:11-32).

So if a good Christian spouse is a gift from God, and God often removes his favor from people who are walking in rebellion against him, it's also safe to assume that those who walk in rebellion could miss out on the spouse God has for them or delay a healthy marriage from starting as soon as it could have.

Often times people may want to blame God for their singleness (Proverbs 19:2-3), but if they spent their college years living in sin, spent their twenties living in more sin, and then get to their thirties and want to be married to a great Christian spouse, that might not happen the way they want. It's never right to be mad at God, especially when our life is simply a reflection of our poor choices.

Rather than get mad, we must remember that God's grace never runs out (Romans 5:20). God will always forgive us when we truly confess our sins to him (1 John 1:9). He is eager to turn what was meant for evil into good (Genesis 50:20). While there's breath in your lungs there's time to repent (Isaiah 55:6).

I don't know why you may be single. It might just be God's plan for you right now, or it might be because of your own sin. If your singleness is caused by your sinfulness, the best action to take is to immediately repent to God. Ask him to forgive you. Ask him to help you change. And then do what the Bible commands, listen to the Holy Spirit, repent when you make mistakes, and obey God with all the might he gives you.

**The Bible Says to Seek God in Your Singleness, No Matter What Caused This Season**

Again, don't instantly assume because you are single God is disciplining you for your sin. The bigger point to make here is this: whether your singleness is a consequence of your sin or it's just God's plan for you not to be married yet, God wants you to serve and love him right now.

In the big picture, it doesn't really matter if your singleness is a consequence for your sin or not. Your path should be the same no matter why you are single – seek God in your singleness.

He can redeem any situation. No blessing is too hard or big for God to give. View your singleness as a gift from God, even if it started out as a consequence. God disciplines those he loves (Hebrews 12:6).

God uses everything for his glory. Love him, follow him, and you will experience God's will for your life.

# Study Questions

1. Does singleness feel like a blessing or a curse to you? What does the Bible say?

2. Why does God remove his favor from our lives sometimes? Have you ever experienced a season like this?

3. What is God teaching you through this chapter? What emotions, questions, or comments arose in you as you read this?

(Note: It's okay if you disagree with some of what was said in this chapter or will read in the chapters ahead. Unpack what you believe and just make sure it's rooted in Scripture.)

# Chapter 2

# 4 Truths to Help You Know If God Is Calling You to a Life of Singleness

Perhaps one of the most prevalent questions amongst single Christians is, "How will I know if God wants me to get married or remain single?" Marriage is a big deal to God. Marriage is central to reflecting the gospel (Ephesians 5:22-33), it is the way God has ordained the human race to be populated (Genesis 1:28), and thus most Christians are called to be married.

There are many Christians, however, who are called to singleness. So how will you know if God is calling you to a life of singleness?

## You May Be Called By God to Singleness If You Know Your Whole Focus Should Be on Ministry

Often times the church you attend values marriage or singleness more than the other. The Bible makes clear, however, that both marriage and singleness are equally important callings from God. 1 Corinthians 7:38 states, "So then he who marries his betrothed does well, and he who refrains from marriage will do even better."

At first glance, 1 Corinthians 7:38 seems to totally disprove my statement that marriage and singleness are equally important callings from God. Notice, though, that this verse begins with "So." Paul says that those who choose the calling of singleness "do even better" because in 1 Corinthians 7:29-35, Paul explains that the value of singleness is that you can focus solely on God. He goes as far to say, "From now on, let those who have wives live as though they had none" ( 1 Corinthians 7:29).

Clearly Paul is not saying that husbands should abandon their wives and families to serve the Lord. The point of this passage is that whether you are married or single, your goal should be to serve the Lord with the same focus as someone who is single because they have committed their life to serving the Lord. This is why he said in 1 Corinthians 7:38 that those who choose Christian singleness have done better.

It's not better to be single rather than married. It is better, however, that you seek to serve the Lord and not have other distractions. So if you choose singleness for this reason, singleness is better for you. But to deny your calling of marriage would be to dishonor the Lord. If you are called to marriage, then it would not be better for you to be single. The big takeaway is this:

> *If you are called to marriage, you must seek to serve the Lord with the same passion that you would have if you were a Christian called to singleness.*

Paul qualified his statements when he declared, "I wish that all were as I myself am [single]. But each has his own gift from God, one of one kind and one of another" (1 Corinthians 7:7).

So one way you will know if God is calling you to singleness is if your motivation is simply to serve the Lord. If you have a desire to live a Christian life of singleness because you hate men, don't want to submit to a husband, don't want the responsibility of caring for a wife, don't want to deal with all the emotional wounds you experienced because of your parents' failed marriage, don't want to stop dating multiple people – if your desire to remain single is rooted in anything other than to please the Lord, this is not a sign that you are called to singleness.

## If You Don't "burn with passion"/Sexual Desires, God May Be Calling You to Singleness

"Does God want me to be single forever?" One sign that will help you determine if God wants you to be single is if he completely takes away your sexual desires. Again, it is crucial to make sure your feelings and desires are not rooted in unhealthy wounds. For example, if you don't have a sexual desire because you were sexually abused as a child, this is not a sign you are called to singleness.

If, however, you are seeking to love God and deal with the wounds of your past but you simply don't have a strong sexual drive, this may be a sign that God wants you to be single forever. God does not want you to be single if you burn with sexual passion. 1 Corinthians 7:1-2, 8-9 explains:

> "Now concerning the matters about which you wrote: "It is good for a man not to have sexual relations with a woman." But because of the temptation to sexual immorality, each man should have his own wife and each woman her own husband. . . . To the unmarried and the widows I say that it is good for them to remain single as I am. But if they cannot exercise self-control, they should marry. For it is better to marry than to burn with passion."

None of this means that just because you have a sexual desire it is a guarantee you will one day be married. God's ways and plans for us are sometimes not that clear. God knows what he's doing, but he doesn't always reveal everything so clearly to us when we want to know. If you do have a sexual desire, however, this is good biblical evidence that you should pursue marriage.

**Religious Reasons Will Not Help You Know If God Is Calling You to Christian Singleness**

Marriage is a gift from God. Marriage should never disqualify anyone from any type of godly ministry. Sadly, there are many religions today that claim celibacy and singleness are requirements for holiness. 1 Timothy 4:1-5 explains:

> "Now the Spirit expressly says that in later times some will depart from the faith by devoting themselves to deceitful spirits and teachings of demons, through the insincerity of liars whose consciences are seared, who forbid marriage and require abstinence from foods that God created to be received with thanksgiving by those who believe and know the truth. For everything created by God is good, and nothing is to be rejected if it is received with thanksgiving, for it is made holy by the word of God and prayer."

If you want to serve the Lord, this is not a sign that you are called by God to singleness. God can call you to marriage or singleness and call you to serve him in full-time ministry as well. While many Christian religions like Catholicism certainly do many good things for God's kingdom, their teaching on priestly celibacy is simply unbiblical.

**Love God and He Will Reveal His Calling on You, Whether It's Marriage or Christian Singleness**

You may not be able to know right now if God wants you to stay single forever. Most of the time God does not give us signs that would reveal his whole plan for our lives all at once.

Rather than spend your whole life seeking signs on whether or not God has called you to marriage or singleness, the wiser approach is to do what you know God has called you to do.

We all know God has called all Christians to love him and other people. When we simply seek the Lord with all of our hearts, God will reveal the next part of his calling for us when we need to know it. Ultimately each Christian simply needs to seek the Lord, submit to his word, and obey what he or she feels led to do.

Marriage and singleness are both wonderful callings from God. If you desire to be married and not remain single forever, odds are God has not called you to singleness. Only God truly knows what his plan for you is, so seek the Lord and in due time he will make it all clear.

God may want you to be single or he may want you to be married . . . we don't know for sure. But we do know he definitely wants you to serve and love him right now.

## Study Questions

1. What are some biblical indicators that someone may be called to a life of singleness? What Bible verses support these indicators?

2. What is the main benefit to Christian singleness? Why does Paul say that even married people are to act as though they were unmarried (1 Corinthians 7:29)?

3. How does marriage glorify God? How does singleness glorify God?

# Chapter 3

# How to Love the Opposite Sex During Your Season of Singleness

*"This is my command: Love each other in the same way I have loved you. There is no greater love than to lay down one's life for one's friend." -John 15:12-13 (NLT)*

How can a Christian single love those of the opposite sex well? To properly answer this important question, the first thing you must do is define your definition of love. The truest essence of love is expressed in the words and actions of Jesus (John 15:13), "There is no greater love than to lay down one's life for one's friend."

With John 15:13 in mind, the basic explanation of love is this: true love is choice. Love is not just a feeling, an emotion, or a specific set of actions, though it involves these things. In its simplest form love is the choice to put another person above yourself.

The level to which you put another person above yourself is the measure of how much you are expressing love to them. This is why the greatest love you can have is to sacrifice your life for another. When you do this, you are putting them above yourself to the greatest measure you are able. But to love someone well, you don't have to physically die for them. You just have to put them above yourself. In this way you are "laying down [your] life" for them. You are forfeiting your rights for the needs of another. This is what love does.

The way you love other single people is by putting them above yourself, above your own needs and desires. This means that in every situation, you need to ask yourself, "Are my actions self-motivated or love motivated?" There is nothing wrong with finding joy or pleasure because of another person.

The problem occurs when your plan to fulfill your own needs begins to infringe on the wellbeing of another person.

It's far too common for single people to cross emotional lines without any proper commitment because they are trying to fill themselves in ways only God or their future spouse should. Most people know it is unloving to cross sexual lines, but did you know there's such a thing as an emotional promiscuity as well? It is unloving to relationally orbit around another person, taking emotional energy from them without any intention to commit further.

The level of your closeness with someone should match your level of commitment. This is why certain things (like sex, living together, etc.) should only be done in marriage. Marriage is the biggest commitment a human can make to another human, therefore these two have rights with each other that should not be given outside of marriage. You should not bare all of your heart, dreams, and emotions with someone who is not your spouse because the level of commitment will be absent. Commitment and intimacy must always go hand in hand if you want to be healthy and protect your heart.

To love the opposite sex well, you must try and protect their heart. For some, this might mean you call and text less, making sure you don't send the wrong signal if you have no romantic interest in them. For others, this might mean you keep calling and texting but you start committing too, entering into an exclusive dating relationship with this person to see if this is the person God has for you. Each situation will be different; you will have to learn to walk with Jesus and learn to be aware of how your self-motivated actions can negatively affect the opposite sex.

In short, single Christian men and women should go to each other to offer rather than to take. This basically means you stop idolizing the opposite sex and you stop going to them to find your value as a person. This means that you learn to find your worth and acceptance in Jesus Christ and him alone, not in other people or in what they think of you.

Going to singles of the opposite sex in service rather than in need will free you from trying to find your worth and validation as a person in the opposite sex. It will also better prepare you for marriage if this is God's call for you.

Marriage is not the place where you ultimately go to find your self-worth. You should feel loved in marriage, but marriage will not fill the hole God is meant to fill, just as nothing else will either. Marriage, however, is one of the best places to express you wholeness and love which you find in Jesus. Your acts of service should flow to others out of your love for God and his love for you; marriage is a great place for acts of service, thus it is a great place to allow your relationship with God to be expressed through your service to another human being.

As a single person, you should start training for marriage now by serving your brothers and sisters in Christ rather than seeking to be served by them. If you come into your future marriage with the servant's mindset you gained in your singleness, you will spare yourself tons of marital grief.

The only way you will be able to offer a selfless love like Christ commands, one unmotivated by personal or social-status gain, will be to have all your needs met in God. Then and only then will you be free to lay down your life for people of the opposite sex during your season of singleness like Jesus did.

So how can you love the opposite sex well as a single person? Answer: Love God above everyone else. He'll shoot you straight.

## Study Questions

1. Do you find it complicated to truly love people of the opposite sex during your season of singleness? Is it tempting to try and take rather than give? Why or why not?

2. How can you intentionally love your brothers and sisters in Christ without sending them the wrong message? If you are not interested in a romantic relationship with someone, how can you still love them well?

3. Do you agree that the level of intimacy (sexual and emotional) given should match the level of commitment given too? Why or why not?

# Chapter 4

## Why Does God Wait to Bless Us?

"God, bless me!" is the common, sometimes subconscious prayer of nearly every heart. It can be prayed in pain, in hopes of relief from some storm in your life, or it can be prayed simply out of a deep, unfulfilled longing within you. It can be a frantic prayer, or one whispered in the night as you kneel quietly by your bedside. However it's prayed, for whatever reason it's prayed, every honest human heart can relate to this longing prayer.

So why does God wait to bless us sometimes? I mean, if God is really the God he claims to be, he can do anything . . . right? He could grant the new car, heal every sickness, grant wealth, and, most importantly for our study in this book, he could grant the perfect spouses so many keep praying for. All of the desires of our hearts could be fulfilled if God would just bless us . . . right?

As we are all aware through the process of trial and error, God does not always conform to our prayers. He doesn't always say "Yes!" to our every request. In humility, we first need to admit that we won't always know why God does or does not do what we want. Sometimes we just need to trust him in faith no matter what he allows or doesn't allow.

But I think we can find some answers to "Why does God wait to bless us?" by studying Deuteronomy 7:9 (NLT) which says God "lavishes his unfailing love on those who love him and obey his commands." From this verse we can draw at least three conclusions.

## God Withholds Blessings to Discourage Our Rebellion

The first conclusion we must take from Deuteronomy 7:9 is that if God is not lavishing his love on us, then we must not love him, which means obeying his commands (I John 5:3). God often waits to bless until we love him well and obey him because to do otherwise would be cruel.

If he lavished his love on a rebellious sinner, what good would that do his child, the object of his affections? He would spoil us right into an eternity in hell if he blessed us with everything we wanted while letting us be content without him. He knows only he can save us from the consequences of our sins, which is death (Romans 6:23); therefore, if he let us be content in disobedience to him, we would never turn to him and be saved.

In addition to this, God knows that if we do not have him as the Lord of our lives, we will simply turn every blessing he gives us into an idol, which will then curse our lives rather than bless our lives. Only when we are rightly aligned with God will we be full enough to not turn good things into ultimate things. When we are without God, we are searching for a replacement god. Thus God often times withholds good blessings because he knows we will worship them rather than him. Never is this truer than when it comes to relationships with the opposite sex. God loves us too much to bless us with idols, thus he waits to bless us until we love him.

Of course in many ways God does bless us even while we are living in active sin (Romans 5:8, Matthew 5:45). But if you are living a sinful lifestyle, you can be assured God is withholding many massive blessings he desires to give you.

## God Waits to Bless Us Until We Love Him Because Loving Him Is the Blessing

Why does God wait to bless us? The second conclusion we can make from Deuteronomy 7:9 when answering this question is that to love and obey the Lord is the real blessing in itself. Perhaps he "lavishes his love on those who love him and obey his commands" because that's the nature of loving and obeying God. Perhaps God has not commanded us to love him for his good, but for our good.

As it says in Jeremiah 32:39 (NLT), "And I will give them one heart and one purpose: to worship me forever, for their own good and for the good of all their descendants." The greatest gift God could ever give us was to create us to worship him. He knows he's the best thing ever. He's not being prideful, he's just being honest. As C.S. Lewis said, "God cannot give us a happiness and peace apart from Himself, because it is not there. There is no such thing."

Therefore God waits to bless us until we love and obey him because loving and obeying him is the blessing he always desires to give.

No relationship, worldly position, or blessing of any sort can fill us like a love-relationship with God. He's the greatest. Nothing else could be greater. Therefore, he knows he can fill us the best. He would never make us for a lesser god.

It says in Psalms 37:4, "Delight yourself in the Lord, and he will give you the desires of your heart." He will give us our heart's deepest desires when we delight in him because that is our heart's deepest desire – to delight in the Lord.

When we turn completely to him, we will find that we have no unmet desire, ". . . for I have learned how to be content with whatever I have. . . . For I can do everything through Christ, who gives me strength" (Philippians 4: 11-13).

Out of his love for us, God made us to need one thing above every other thing: himself.

## God Waits to Bless Us Until His Blessings Will Truly Benefit Us

Although God himself is the greatest blessing God desires to give, this does not mean he is the only blessing he gives. God does bless his people with good things like spouses, money, food, houses, clothes, friendships, restful vacations, and the list could go on forever.

So why does God wait to bless us with these types of things? Deuteronomy 7:9 says God always lavishes his love on those who love him. Therefore if you are really loving and obeying God and yet you still do not have what you are specifically asking for, the only reason left is that to bless you with that specific request would be unloving.

God promises to bless his children with good gifts (Matthew 7:11), but only God truly knows what will be good for us. God promises to lavish his love on us, but only he knows what will be loving for each one of us in our specific context. Love is not doing what someone wants. Love is doing what is best for someone no matter the cost to yourself or the person you love.

Imagine how cruel it would be if God always answered our every prayer. What if God answered the prayer of every high school student who prayed that he or she will marry this or that specific person? What if God always gave you the job you thought you wanted? What if God always said "yes" even when doing so would cause you to endure so much pain that you never could have expected because you can't see into the future like God?

God often times waits to bless us because what we think will be a blessing will actually end up being a curse to us. For example: You probably won't know in high school what kind of spouse would be best for you, thus in love God kindly often times does not answer these high school prayers. One of the most amazing blessings in my own marriage is that Bethany and I continually change as we grow older, and yet out marriage continues to be strong. God has placed me with a woman that is changing while I too change, and yet we are still amazingly compatible. God alone can give you a spouse who will be a blessing not just when you first get married, but as you both change year to year. In our humanness, we could never factor these types of variables into the equation.

God only blesses us with things that will benefit us. Therefore if you are not living in sin and you really love God and yet you don't have something you keep asking God for, like a spouse, the safest conclusions is that what you are asking for would not be good for you right now.

You can trust God. He always has your best interest in mind. Ask him what would need to change in you so that what you are seeking would be beneficial. For example, often times people pray for a spouse so hard and yet don't get one because they are not ready to be married. Ask God why you're not ready. What negative quality is in you that would ruin your marriage if God gave it to you right now? Sometimes, when we repent of something in ourselves through his grace, it frees God to bless us with a gift he's wanted to give us all along.

Just before I started dating my wife, God took me through a season just like this. I asked him, "Lord, what is in me that is hindering you from blessing me?" When he brought certain things to my attention, I worked on them. I also began praying that God would prepare my future wife's heart. I'm not saying these prayers caused God to bring Bethany and I together when he did. Perhaps he brought me through this season and led me to pray these prayers in preparation for the season he already had preplanned for me. Either way, it was massively beneficial and I know my dating season, engagement, and marriage would have been much tougher if I did not ask God these specific questions.

Ultimately, God wants only the best for his children, and he knows he's the best. God wants only what will never fail for his children, and he knows only he will never fail us. God wants only the greatest love for his children, and he knows only he is perfect and full of the greatest love.

Therefore God waits to bless until the blessing will draw us closer to him.

# Study Questions

1. If you are someone who wants to be married, what are some possible reasons God has not blessed you with a spouse yet? Is it just not your time? Is he calling you to do something specific that would be better accomplished in your singleness right now?

2. Why does God sometimes wait to bless us with certain things until we love and obey him?

3. Have you ever prayed for something only to later thank God that he did not answer that prayer? Why should we trust that even when God says "No" to something we ask for, he is still showing us maximum love like he always does?

# Chapter 5

## 4 Reasons You Should Not Feel Guilty About Being Discontent "With" Singleness

Some Christians are called to singleness. These types of people are typically quite content with not being in a romantic relationship, they don't struggle with sexual temptation, and their desire for singleness is rooted in their desire to serve God.

Most Christians who are single, however, don't fall into this category. The vast majority of us have not been blessed with the gift of singleness. One lie churches often unintentionally teach Christian singles is that it's not okay to be discontent with their singleness.

Through well-meant teachings and seminars on how Christian singles must find all their contentment in Christ, people often end up feeling guilty for being unhappy about their lack of marriage. Many people feel it is wrong to want to be married.

### The Bible Says It Is Good to Want to Be Married

The Bible, however, does not condemn the desire to be married. If you hope to be married, it is natural and good to be discontent with your singleness. The danger is when you allow yourself to be discontent with Christ.

Through Christ, we can be content "in" every situation (Philippians 4:12-13), even our unwanted singleness. But that does not mean we must be content "with" every situation. Your heart must find its ultimate and total joy in Christ. But even in your joy with Christ, you can be unhappy with your circumstance. You only sin when you allow your unwanted circumstances to affect your joy in Christ. Unwanted circumstances should increase and not decrease your joy in Christ. The more we see the imperfections in this world, the more we should value the perfections of Christ.

So if you are someone who wishes to be married, you don't have to deny this desire. You can be honest with God. You can be vulnerable with him.

Often times people think God will bless them with a spouse when they no longer want one, as though God thinks it's sinful of you to pursue marriage and thus will only bless you when you stop sinning by stopping your marriage search.

While God wants you to love him above everything else, he also says marriage is a good desire, "He who finds a wife finds a good thing and obtains favor from the LORD" (Proverbs 18:22).

### It's Not Wrong to Want to Be Married Because God Wants Us to Care About Real-Life Circumstances

While God wants us to be content in every situation, this does not mean we must become blind to real needs in the world and in our own lives.

Idolizing marriage or allowing your desire to find a spouse overtake your desire to love God is sinful. But you can love God completely and still desire your circumstances to change. Christianity does emphasize the need to be content with every situation. Christians are told to work towards change while also being joyful in Christ even if change doesn't happen. No matter what is happening in life, we must find total contentment in Christ.

To seek an inner tranquility with a total blindness to our actual life circumstances is closer to Buddhism that Christianity. In Buddhism the goal is reach a state of nirvana, which is a mental state of being that blocks out and ignores the world as you "clear your mind" and focus on nothing. This is not Christianity.

For example, the book of Philippians is a book all about finding joy in Christ despite the external struggles the world throws at us. Throughout the book, you will find Bible verses like these:

"Whatever happens, conduct yourselves in a manner worthy of the gospel of Christ." (Philippians 1:27)

"Do everything without grumbling or arguing . . . ." (Philippians 2:14)

"But even if I am being poured out like a drink offering on the sacrifice and service coming from your faith, I am glad and rejoice with all of you. So you too should be glad and rejoice with me." (Philippians 2:17-18)

"Finally, my brothers, rejoice in the Lord." (Philippians 3:1)

"But whatever gain I had, I counted as loss for the sake of Christ. Indeed, I count everything as loss because of the surpassing worth of knowing Christ Jesus my Lord." (Philippians 3:7-8)

"Rejoice in the Lord always; again I will say, rejoice. . . . Not that I am speaking of being in need, for I have learned in whatever situation I am to be content. I know how to be brought low, and I know how to abound. In

any and every circumstance, I have learned the secret of facing plenty and hunger, abundance and need. I can do all things through him who strengthens me."
(Philippians 4:4, 11-13)

But even though Paul instructs us to find joy in Christ and not our circumstances, he also has a healthy anxiety over the wellbeing of his coworker who became ill (Philippians 2:25-30). Even though Paul found that through Christ he had all he needed, he also requested that provisions be made for him by the Philippians (Philippians 4:16-20). And although he learned to find the good in false preachers who still preached Christ (Philippians 1:17-18), he also warned us to stay away from people like that (Romans 16:17-20).

Likewise, Jesus knew that he was going to raise Lazarus from the dead. He knew that it was going to turn out well. Jesus' joy was always perfect in God. But that doesn't mean he didn't weep for Lazarus still. When John 11:35 says, "Jesus wept" it shows us Jesus' perfect humanness. Jesus is God, but he is human too – perfectly both. And thus Jesus wept, because to be human is to actually care about things on earth. God really cares about the details of our human lives (1 Peter 5:7), thus to reflect him as image bearers, we must care about the details too.

Again, humans are made in the image of God, and God really cares about the actual circumstances in your life (Matthew 6:8, 32-33). Thus our pursuit of being authentically human reflections of God as he originally intended does not mean we need perfect contentment "with" our circumstances. We must seek perfect contentment in Christ so we can be content in him while we are in any circumstance.

Nowhere in the Bible are we told we must enjoy unwanted circumstances. We are told, rather, to enjoy Christ even in unwanted circumstances.

## It Is Not Wrong to Want to Be Married Because God Designed This Need in Us

What's my point here? The point is that it's not sinful to want to be married. It's okay if you are content with your singleness, but it is equally fine if you are not. You don't need to be content "with" your singleness as long as you are content with Christ "in" your singleness.

Your joy must be found in Christ. No circumstance, no matter how good, will ever fill your heart's need for God. But there are lesser needs within the heart that God gave humans which are found outside of God himself.

He said of Adam that it was not good for him to be alone (Genesis 2:18), and this was before sin entered the picture. This means that even though Adam had God fully, God still created Adam to need a wife.

Eve was never to usurp or challenge God's place in Adam's life. But in love God blessed humans with the opportunity to enjoy symbols and lesser expressions of him that are not God himself. God made us to desire blessings that are not God.

All these good gifts come from God (James 1:17). And, yes, all good in the world is a reflection of God that should make us want the source of that reflection more. All our pursuits of the gifts should remind us of the Giver of those gifts. So even in your desire for a spouse, it should enhance your desire and pleasure in God.

But to desire a spouse and love him or her is good. To want a spouse is not an expression of your lack of joy in Christ.

## Don't Feel Guilty For Wanting a Spouse. Seek Christ and Find Joy in Him

You don't need to feel guilty for wanting a spouse. You should only feel guilty if your desires are crowding out your desire for God. He wants to walk with you through the pain, trials, and unwanted circumstances. It's okay if you are not happy with your singleness as long as you are still happy in Christ.

The Christian life can be beautifully summarized by 2 Corinthians 6:10, "we are sorrowful, yet always rejoicing." It's okay if your singleness is unwanted and thus you have a sorrow in your heart, as long as within that same heart you are always rejoicing in Christ.

One day perfect circumstances and perfect contentment in Christ will collide. But before the time when God makes all things new, we can still find contentment in Christ even with unwanted circumstances.

# Study Questions

1. What is the difference between being content "with" a circumstance compared to being content "in" a circumstance?

2. Do you think you will ever have enough earthly blessings to find total fulfillment? What is the only way we will find lasting joy?

3. Do you think some churches or Christian leaders make singles feel guilty in any ways that are unbiblical? Explain some of the good or bad experiences you've had in relation to this question.

# Section 2

# How to Thrive During Your Season of Singleness

# Chapter 6

## Are You Dating or Married to God?

The difference between teen romance and a deeply committed marriage is persevering faithfulness. When you date, you are gauging whether or not you want to remain with that person. When you get married, your only thought is to remain, love, and be faithful no matter what happens.

Likewise, to be Christian, you must move past the dating season and fully commit to your marriage with God.

Throughout church history there has been a debate on whether or not one can lose their salvation. It is my belief that the most biblical stance is that once you are truly saved you cannot lose your salvation, but if you reject Christ without repentance it simply means you were never truly saved to begin with (1 John 2:19). Thus the true evidence that someone is saved is their perseverance (Colossians 1:22-23, Romans 11:22).

God made marriage to be a visible representation of his relationship with his church. When we are truly saved, we are joined to God like a husband and wife is joined together. God, therefore, rejects the idea of divorce in earthly marriages because this does not accurately represent the faithfulness he gives and expects in his marriage to his people. The only reason God allows divorce is when adultery occurs (Matthew 5:31-32). Likewise, the only thing that proves our marriage with God was never real in the first place is when our hearts find another lover and it never returns to God.

Therefore, we must ask ourselves, are we keeping our marriage vows to God? Traditional Christian vows read as:

I _____, take you _____ to be my lawful
wedded spouse, to have and to hold from this day
forward, for better, for worse, for richer, for poorer, in
sickness and in health, to love and to cherish, according
to God's holy decree, and I pledge my faithfulness as
long as we both shall live.

The clear emphasis of these vows is faithfulness no matter
what happens. We need never question God's faithfulness to
us, but everyone should always take an honest look at their
own faithfulness to God (Hebrews 3:12). For if we find
ourselves constantly running from our Spouse whenever
something unpleasurable happens, then perhaps we never made
our true vows to God in the first place.

Of course we will fail and sin over and over again, but do we
come back, showing our faithfulness despite personal failure?
Do we run when times are worse, run when times are poorer,
run when we are sick, therefore not pledging our faithfulness
forever?

We all must ask ourselves if we are the type of person who acts
like teenagers dating, hanging around only when times with
God are superficial and bubbly, wanting only the quick
pleasures without the commitment? Or are we like that faithful
old couple who has been married for years, sticking with God
through all the peaks and valleys, births and deaths, job
promotions and job losses, and through all the strife that occurs
relationally because of our own sinfulness?

An earthly marriage between husband and wife expects nothing
less than these basic vows being met. It hopes for more, but it
cannot survive with less. Notice there is no promise of
perfection in Christian marriage vows, only a promise that their
hearts will never be given to anyone other than their spouse.

You won't be perfect in your relationship with God, but you must always persevere. May we be faithful as he has been faithful, not falling for a soft version of Christianity that allows for dating God rather than settling down and marrying him forever.

## Study Questions

1. How does teen romance not reflect Christ's relationship with his church? How does a committed marriage reflect Christ and his church?

2. Think of a marriage that you admire. What is it about this couple that you believe makes them special? How does their love reflect God's love for his church? If you can't think of anyone, imagine a healthy marriage and describe the qualities you believe would be present.

3. If you had to summarize traditional Christian marriage vows, how would you state them in your own words? What types of promises are made? What types of promises are not made?

# Chapter 7

## Don't Waste It: 7 Ways to Use Your Christian Singleness

Getting married changes everything. The hope is that it changes your life for the better, but the guarantee is that marriage will change you no matter what.

One of the most obvious ways that marriage changes your life is through the sharing, responsibility, and commitments that come along with "I do." In other words, you have less free time.

By "free time" I don't mean all the other time is "slave time." I just mean that the more commitments you have to people (spouse, kids, job, church, relatives, friends, est.), the less time you have to pursue other desires. Getting married opens Pandora's Box when it comes to your commitments.

When you get married, you instantly inherit another set of relatives, another set of friends, and another set of coworkers Marriage usually leads to having kids. Having kids usually means getting a bigger house. Getting a bigger house means you need to work more to pay for that house. On and on it goes.

I'm sure you've heard a married person lament, "I remember how much time I had when I was single." This doesn't mean just because you're single you have no life. Being single doesn't mean you're not busy. But ask anyone who's married, especially if they have kids, and most of them will tell you they had way more free time when they were unmarried. Paul says,

"I want you to be free from anxieties. The unmarried man is anxious about the things of the Lord, how to please the Lord. But the married man is anxious about worldly things, how to please his wife, and his interests are divided. And the unmarried or betrothed woman is anxious about the things of the Lord, how to be holy in body and spirit. But the married woman is anxious about worldly things, how to please her husband. I say this for your own benefit, not to lay any restraint upon you, but to promote good order and to secure your undivided devotion to the Lord." (1 Corinthians 7:32-35)

Most of us are not called to a life of singleness, but all of us are called not to waste our life during our singleness. Jesus said that those who are given much, much will be required (Luke 12:48). God doesn't want you to waste your singleness by waiting around to get married. And when you get married, you don't want to look back on all the things you could have done, on all the things you should have learned, or on all the people you could have served.

It is so easy to waste your singleness. So here are 7 ways you can use your Christian singleness while you have it. (These are in no particular order and this is definitely not an exhaustive list.)

#### #1: Personal Growth

When you're single, you have a lot more time to think about yourself. And I don't mean that in a bad way. After childhood and high school, not to mention your 20's and 30's, you are going to get wounded. Whether it's through your parents' divorce, an unstable home life, a rebellious streak, or some other wounding agent, we all have areas in our hearts that need healing.

It's always much more ideal to do this soul work when you're single. We'll constantly be growing throughout life, but if you never take the time to do some meaningful reflection on your inner health when you're single, odds are you won't when you get into a relationship either.

On a less spiritual note, singleness provides an amazing opportunity to pursue the career and education goals that you have in life. You can pursue that degree when you're married with kids, but I guarantee when you get to that season of life you will wish you would have not wasted all the time you had during your singleness. If you have ambition for something, set yourself up for long-term success by putting in the work when it's more convenient.

Pursuing your goals and doing soul work will never be convenient, but it is more convenient when you are single. Don't waste this opportunity.

## #2: Get to Know God Really Well

While this list is in no particular order, this is the most important way you can use your singleness. Growing in our personal relationship with God is something that must take precedence in every season of life. But during your season of singleness, you have an amazing opportunity to set a firm faith foundation for the rest of your life.

If you don't read the Bible or other books about God now, you probably are not going to later. If you just can't find the time to join that small group as a single person, odds are you won't when you're married either. If you reject the Holy Spirit's urge to wake up early to pray before work during this season, it's unlikely you will obey his prompting in the next season either.

The greatest biblical benefit of singleness is that it provides a season of life that will give you the best opportunity to focus on God (1 Corinthians 7:32-35). It's never going to be easier to set aside time to spend with Jesus than it is during your season of singleness.

None of this means that marriage should cause us to pursue Jesus less (1 Corinthians 7:29). It just means that it will be easier (time wise) to pursue Jesus when you don't have other huge relational commitments. Your years of Christian singleness will not be wasted if you use this time to pursue Jesus intimately.

### #3: Develop Your Interpersonal Skills Through Meaningful Friendships

One of the most practical reasons for our season of singleness is interpersonal development. In America, people have choices when it comes to marriage. This is obviously a good thing . . . unless your social skills are horrible (joking).

I know a lot of single men who would really benefit from a wife, because, for example, she would help them realize things like showering, grooming, and showing up on time help you get ahead in life. I know a lot of single women who would benefit from a husband, because, for example, he would show her how offensive she comes across when she unknowingly starts to mother other grown adults.

The problem is that without a spouse, a lot of these types of imbalances will never change. And the more odd and imbalanced you are, the less likely you are to find a spouse. So what can be done?

Friendship is the next best way to develop your interpersonal skills. As a Christian single person you should have your close friends, but you should also be open to meeting all different types of people (men and women). Not only will this be fun (and helpful if you want to find a spouse), but it will also help you become a well-rounded social individual.

Not all people who were homeschooled are weird. But I think we all know a few. Why are they like that? Because they were not exposed to as many other people, which directly affected their social development.

So how can you use your Christian singleness? Use your season of singleness to develop your interpersonal skills.

#### #4: Build a Healthy Support System of Friends and Family

One of the biggest misconceptions about marriage is that your spouse will fill all your relational needs. But your spouse is just that, your spouse. He or she is not your mom, dad, sister, brother, best friend of the same sex, or caring mentor who's been in your shoes before. We need all of these types of people in life.

If you get married, a spouse should be your closest and best confidante. But he or she can't be all that you need relationally. And not to mention you are eventually going to have marriage snafus. Who will you turn to when you need to talk to someone about your relationship with your spouse? Counselors are helpful, but they don't need to be your go-to-person whenever you have a marriage issue.

Develop a strong support system when you are single because you will most likely have the time (at least more time than when you get married) to invest the energy it will take to develop this well rounded, relationship network. Don't waste your singleness on social media, in front of the TV, or hanging out with the same three friends from grade school. Meet people!

Lastly, there is no guarantee you will get married. If you waste your 20's and 30's never making good friends, it only gets harder as time goes on because other people are likely getting married. Being single at a younger age is the easiest time to make lasting friendships because everyone else has more time too. Then when people get older, they can enjoy the close friendships they built earlier in life rather than try to build these friendships later in life, which takes way more effort because married people generally have less time.

It's not impossible to make great friends later in life, but it is more likely when you are younger and single. If you waste your singleness, you will be wasting opportunities to build lifelong friendships.

### #5: Go On Purposeful Missions/Adventures

Spring break vacation with your friends is cool . . . I guess, if you're into that kind of thing. But odds are it will not change your life, develop you as a person, give you lifelong memories, or really help other people in need.

Mission trips, on the other hand, can be fun, adventurous, and a great time with your friends. And they also give you the opportunity to impact the world for Christ in powerful ways. Mission trips break us out of our bubbles and open our eyes to how big God is and how much the world needs him.

You can see beautiful places, you can go on adventures in foreign lands, and you can spend a lot of time helping people all by going on a mission's trip. I met my wife while serving for seven months in Liberia. It was an experience I'll never forget and it changed my walk with God forever.

I've been rock climbing, sky diving, whitewater rafting, backpacking, and on many other adventures. I encourage you to have fun during you singleness. Experience God on these types of adventures too. But there are few better ways to use your singleness that going on an adventure that has purpose, and mission trips provide this opportunity (especially overseas trips).

#### #6: Be Spontaneous

When you're single, try to say "Yes" more than "No" when you get invited to do something positive with other people. Almost all of the things we've talked about so far in this list are severely hampered by being a homebody. Hey, I get it. I've always been more introverted than extroverted. But thankfully God gave me the conviction during my singleness to take advantage of my lack of responsibilities.

Looking back, I didn't do it perfectly, but I don't have regrets revolving around "I wish I did more." My wife was the same way. She really took advantage of her singleness. Now that God has put us together, even though we have less time, we are better equipped to live an adventurous, purposeful life.

Without our years of singleness being spent well, I know this would not be the case.

## #7: Be Intentional, Prayerful, and Prepare for Your Future

In closing, the last piece of advice I can give you is be intentional about how you use your singleness. How you spend your days will be how you spend your life. If we are not careful, we will waste it on stupid luxuries and little pleasures that are gone in an instant.

If you want to avoid wasting your Christian singleness, you will have to be intentional. This list is just the tip of the iceberg. The most important thing is that you are following God's will for your singleness.

What's he asking you to do during this season? Pray about it. Prepare now so you are ready to embrace the future God has for you. We must enjoy the present, but not at the expense of God's future for us. God's way allows us to enjoy the present and prepare for the future.

Use your singleness. Don't let it use you. When you are married and have a few kids (or you are still single a few years from now) you'll be able to look back and thank God for how he prepared you for the seasons you'll be in then. If you don't waste your singleness, I guarantee you will reap the rewards.

*"Do not be deceived: God is not mocked, for whatever one sows, that will he also reap. For the one who sows to his own flesh will from the flesh reap corruption, but the one who sows to the Spirit will from the Spirit reap eternal life. And let us not grow weary of doing good, for in due season we will reap, if we do not give up. So then, as we have opportunity, let us do good to everyone, and especially to those who are of the household of faith." –Galatians 6:7-10*

## Study Questions

1. Do you feel like you have used your singleness well so far? Why or why not? What changes can you make so you don't repeat some of the same mistakes?

2. Which of the seven things listed here stuck out to you? Why?

3. Spend some time in prayer and reflection and ask God how he wants you to use your singleness. What do you feel led to do? Write some specific things down so you can come back to this list when you need to refocus.

# Chapter 8

# How to Deal With Unmet Expectations

Expectations and desires are such a beautiful and yet dangerous part of life. To have a dream creates a feeling in your heart that is essential for a meaningful life. To have desires is to have a heart that is alive. If you feel nothing, hope for nothing, or never have a dream, it probably means you have lost your heart and passion for life.

But how do we maintain joy when we have unmet expectations, for as the Bible says in Proverbs 13:12, "Hope deferred makes the heart sick, but a desire fulfilled is a tree of life."

## The Bible Says We Must Keep Our Hearts Alive, Even With Unmet Expectations

Everyone who dares to be honest knows deep down there are strong desires in their hearts. Some may want to invent the next cure to a disease, be a mom, be a husband, or to simply make more money to provide for their family. It doesn't take a counselor to know that if these good desires go unmet for too long, it's totally understandable for someone to begin to lose heart, for hope deferred make the heart sick.

Although it is understandable, God does not make it excusable. He instructs through his word, "Guard your heart, for it is the wellspring of life" (Proverbs 4:23). So we have these facts we must make sense of: It's good to have desires, unmet desires will make the heart sick, in life there will be many desires that go unmet, and God expects us to guard our hearts so they don't

get sick. It seems these facts are on an unavoidable collision
course causing us to lose heart and thus disobey God.

**The Bible Says God Must Reign Over All Our Desires,
Including Our Unmet Expectations**

Many times we think the only solution to avoiding a broken
heart is to put an impenetrable wall around our desires. We
think to guard our hearts means to starve our hearts of dreams.
But God does not instruct us to guard our hearts of all desires;
he instructs us to guard our hearts so our desires are placed in
the correct place – ultimately in him. 1 John 5:21 (NLT) states,
"Dear children, keep away from anything that might take
God's place in your hearts."

David had many desires and dreams fulfilled during his
lifetime. One of his most important dreams, however never
came to fruition:

> "Now it was in the heart of David my father to build a
> house for the name of the LORD, the God of Israel. But
> the LORD said to David my father, 'Whereas it was in
> your heart to build a house for my name, you did well
> that it was in your heart. Nevertheless, you shall not
> build the house, but your son who shall be born to you
> shall build the house for my name.'" (1 Kings 8:17-19)

If David's ultimate desire was to build God a temple, he would
have been crushed when God said "no." But God did not
condemn David for this desire. He actually said that although
David was not the one to build the temple, it was good of
David to have this desire. David's desire was unmet but his
heart did not grow sick. Why? Because although he desired to
build a temple, this was not his main desire. His main desire
was to please the Lord. God said it was good of David to have

the desire to build the temple even though it would never happen because at the root of this desire was to please God.

David was acting like Jesus when he stated his desire was to not go to the cross but then followed it up with, "yet not my will, but yours be done" (Luke 22:42). Jesus did not lose his heart when his desire to avoid the cross was rejected because his truest desire was to please his Abba.

Jesus brought every desire under the authority of his ultimate desire, which was to glorify his Father.

### If Pleasing God Is Our Ultimate Hope, We Don't Have to Be Crushed By Lesser Unmet Expectations

Even though every desire we have will not be met, God is happy with every desire we have that is rooted in pleasing him. Every Christian has had moments where an idea for ministry came to them and they thought it was certainly from God. Then the ministry never happened, so they either thought the dream wasn't from God or he is just cruel for not fulfilling it.

Clarity comes to our lives when we simplify our desires down to one desire – to please God. So whether the specific dream takes place or not, we can be happy in the root desire to please him no matter how life turns out.

When pleasing God is our greatest hope, then even when the surface details don't pan out our foundation will still remain unshaken. When David was dying and he was preparing for his son Solomon to build God the temple (1 Chronicles 22), David was overcome with joy. He was not sick at heart even though he would never see one of his desires fulfilled because his greatest desire was being fulfilled – God's will being done. It wasn't about building a temple or not building a temple. It was about pleasing God. Notice David's prayer for the people just before he dies:

> "I know, my God, that you test the heart and are pleased with integrity. All these things I have given willingly and with honest intent. And now I have seen with joy how willingly your people who are here have given to you. LORD, the God of our fathers Abraham, Isaac and Israel, keep these desires and thoughts in the hearts of your people forever, and keep their hearts loyal to you." (1 Chronicles 29:17, 18)

As an old man who had spent his whole life walking with God, David shared with us the secret to keeping our hearts alive even when certain desires go unmet. Unmet expectations are difficult to deal with, especially our relational desires regarding marriage, but when our hearts are loyal to God above every other desire, the one desire that matters the most will always be realized – pleasing God.

# Study Questions

1. What do you feel when a desire of yours goes unmet? Do you feel God is holding out on you or that you have done something wrong?

2. How can we keep our hearts alive and have good desires without losing heart if they don't pan out the way we thought they should?

3. Why is it important to pay attention to the root desire behind your relationship desires? Do you want to be married (or single) for God-honoring reasons or for idolatrous reasons? Why does it matter?

# Chapter 9

# Christian Singleness, Loneliness, and 5 Healthy Ways to Respond

Christian singleness can be lonely. You may not feel lonely every moment, every day, or even every week, but most Christian singles really struggle in this area.

What compounds this problem is that some Christians feel ashamed for feeling lonely. "Shouldn't Christ be enough? Am I trying to find my value through relationships? Am I a jealous, shallow person for feeling like it's a jab every time I see a new engagement announcement scroll by in my social media feed? Is my loneliness a sign of weakness?"

Loneliness is not a sin. God didn't design every Christian to be married, but he did design every Christian to live in community with other Christians. Even if you feel called to a life of singleness, it is normal to struggle with loneliness. And if you know you want to be married one day, there is nothing wrong with you if you feel lonely during your season of singleness (Genesis 2:18).

How you respond to your loneliness, however, is where the good or the bad happens. God desires to use loneliness during singleness to draw each Christian closer to him, to develop us in new ways, and to cause us to search out the healthy relationships for which we were designed to have.

What follows is a list of 5 healthy ways to respond to the loneliness that often accompanies Christian singleness.

## #1: Don't Deny Your Loneliness. It Will Only Embitter You

One of the most common ways to deal with loneliness is to simply denying it. "I'm not lonely. I'm fine. I don't need a man to define me." "Lonely? Ha, I'm not lonely! Christ is all I need. Plus, I'm going on too many adventures to date a woman right now. I don't even want to be in a relationship at this point in my life."

There's nothing wrong with statements like these . . . as long as they are true. For many Christian singles, they are just saying this type of stuff because they don't want to deal with the loneliness. If they admit that they really are struggling with being alone, they feel the loneliness will only get worse.

The problem with this tactic is that it builds unhealthy resentment towards the opposite sex, towards your friends in dating or marriage relationships, and towards God. To constantly force your good and normal emotions down, you will feel like you need to avoid and reject everything that might trigger these feelings of loneliness.

So when you meet a Christian guy who is also single, rather than respond to his interest in you, you reject the idea completely as a defense mechanism. When you're best friend get's engaged, you stop hanging out with him because you want to avoid being hurt when you see him experiencing what you desire. Rather than pray about your desire to be married, you neglect this area of your walk with God because you fear what he might say. None of these responses are healthy. Avoiding triggers is no cure to loneliness in Christian singleness.

Denying your loneliness only cuts you off in greater ways from the people God designed you to need. If you deny your loneliness, you will hinder yourself from depending on God in the ways he wants.

**#2: Use Loneliness in Christian Singleness as Motivation to Pursue What God Has Made You For**

Okay, so you are no longer denying the loneliness you feel during your season of Christian singleness. So now what? What are you supposed to do with this loneliness?

Loneliness, along with all other unwanted feelings, is a gift in disguise meant to motivate you. I'm not saying you should desire these gifts. What I am saying is that God has a specific purpose in mind when he allows us to experience difficult feelings like loneliness. If Paul would not have had a thorn in his flesh, he would never have called out to God the way he did nor learned to rely on him for power in weakness (2 Corinthians 12:7-10)

God doesn't want us to be victims to our feelings. He wants us to be motivated by our unwanted feelings. Imagine if you never felt hungry but your body still needed food. I'd say (with no research to back this up) that 99% of us are not disciplined enough to manage our bodies without the natural indicators God has built into our DNA. If we didn't feel thirsty, most of us would forget to drink water. If we didn't feel tired, most of would never sleep. If we didn't feel pain, most of us would not allow our broken bones to heal. Feelings are God's healthy warning signs that we are lacking something we need.

Surely our sinful nature corrupts our emotions and feelings at times so they are out of whack. But much of the time you feel certain ways, like lonely, because you are lacking something you were made to need. Don't ignore the warning signs. Address the issue and seek out whatever you are lacking.

If you feel lonely in your Christian singleness, this means you are lacking something good in your life. Don't try to just stop the warning signs (the feeling of loneliness); address the root issue and the symptoms will go away too.

### #3: Put Forth Effort to Find a Spouse (Go on a date!)

The Bible explains that most Christians are designed for marriage (Genesis 2:18). There certainly are many Christians who will be blessed with the gift of singleness (1 Corinthians 7:7). And just because you are lonely, it doesn't mean you don't have this gift. But for most Christians, prolonged loneliness during singleness is a sign that God has designed you for marriage.

Through many well-meaning Christian leaders, loads of Christian singles feel guilty for being active in the dating process. They feel like they are taking matters into their own hands and not trusting God if they do anything other than pray, go to church, and serve in Christian ways.

Putting forth effort to find a spouse is not sinful. There is nothing wrong with pursuing marriage. Certainly we all need to walk with God and obey his personal leading in our lives. If you've turned the idea of marriage into an idol, a short time of repentance will be healthy. But if God designed you for marriage, which he has for most Christians, you must remember that God expects you to pursue the good things he has designed you to need. If you are thirsty and all you do is pray for water, you are missing the point. Get up and get a drink. God blesses us with good things, but he also expects us to reach out and take hold of those good things. And marriage is a very good thing.

Stop feeling guilty about wanting to change your status from "single" to "in a relationship." Marriage won't solve all your problems if your heart is not right with God, but it's possible to still feel lonely in your Christian singleness even if your heart is right with God. God said it was not good for Adam and Eve to be alone (Genesis 2:18). He made men and women to be in relationship with one another. We must never be overwhelmed by loneliness. We must always seek God to fill us completely. But it is healthy to feel lonely when you lack good human relationships because God made us to need these.

If you're walking with God, it's actually possible to feel lonelier because of your lack of good human relationships. Why? Because when we are right with God, our inner being is purified and thus it's most natural, original cravings are free to be unleashed. A heart fully alive feels everything more passionately – pleasure and pain – because it is alive. A dead heart feels less in general. The healthier you are with Christ, the more your heart will feel things. It's sometimes painful to be so alive in a world with so many problems. But the solution is not to kill our hearts so we feel less. The solution is to keep coming alive, keep pursing Christ, and keep pursuing good, no matter how painful it might be. The pain should motivate us to seek the pleasure for which we were made and are currently lacking.

Perhaps you feel lonely because you are just waiting around for something to change. So let me say this with all the love and affection of an older brother who really cares about your wellbeing. I'm not saying this to be a jerk. I just want to say what many of you might need to hear: Go on a freaking date already!

I hear Christians all the time with complaints like, "I haven't even been on date in five years." When I hear that, I want to challenge that person's victimization. Okay, I know it takes two to be in a relationship, so it's sometimes just out of your control. But if you haven't been on a date in over a year, you're in a season of life where you're prepared to be married, and you want be married, then you need to be more active. You need to take responsibility and stop being so passive. Put yourself out there. Go on a date. Do something different. Don't just complain that you haven't been on a date.

Walk with God and make it happen. Maybe one day I will write a book on all the ways to meet somebody because the possibilities are endless. But here's the thing: You are smart. Pray about it. Put your mind to it. And figure out how to meet new people with the intention of dating. If you are doing these things with a good motive, there's nothing wrong with being proactive. Submit to the truth that God is control; but also realize God expects you to be an active participant in life. It's no different when it comes to dating.

Use your loneliness as fuel. Yes, to seek God first, but to also find the man or woman God probably has for you.

## #4: Supplement Your Lack of a Spouse with Other Good Relationships

Marriage is one of the most significant, deepest relationships a human can experience with another human. But marriage is not the only significant relationship that our hearts were made to need.

If you think marriage is the solution to your loneliness, you'll find you might be even lonelier once you actually get married. Sometimes when we get what we want, we experience a massive let down because we thought it was going to fill us in greater ways than it does.

If you don't have healthy relationships with your family, with friends, with a body of believers (church), with people you are mentoring, with people you are being mentored by, with your local community, with your neighbors, with people who have common interests as you – if you don't have a robust relationship network with all different types of people with different roles to play in your life, you will feel lonely to some degree.

Yes, no matter what you do, you might still feel the sting of loneliness that comes during Christian singleness. But that sting is going to be a lot worse if you're relationships are deficient in other areas of your life too.

Be practical, proactive, and avoid passivity. You might not be able to find a spouse right now. But can you find some more friends? Can you find a good church to serve at with other believers? Can you build deeper relationships with the support system you do have?

The funny thing is that those who have healthy relationships that are not romantic in nature are often the ones who find romantic love sooner. By having a healthy, well balanced relational life, you are becoming a well-rounded person who will be attractive to suitors. If you stay at home all the time, only spend time with your mom, or just hang out with your old high school buddies, odds are you are not developing relationally as you should. These other relationships are the best training for romantic relationships. If you are an underdeveloped community member, friend, brother/sister, or son/daughter, odds are you will be underdeveloped relationally in your future romantic relationships too.

Additionally, by having more relationships that are not romantic in nature, you will also give yourself a greater network of people that will naturally help you find a romantic partner. I'm not saying everyone in life should try to set you up on blind dates. But the more people you know, the more people they will introduce you to. If you have friends at a few churches, and those friends invite you to spend time with their friends, you will meet more people. This just naturally increases your chances of finding someone you are compatible with.

### #5: Use Your Loneliness to Grow With Christ

Well if you've been a Christian and you've read things about singleness for a fair amount of time, you probably expected this point. But don't gloss over it just because you've heard it so many times before and it seems so obvious.

Use your loneliness in Christian singleness to grow with Christ. The greatest blessing singleness offers is a life that is less cluttered and thus more open to spending time with Jesus. Marriage will grow your walk with God too, but singleness has its own unique blessings that you won't have during any other time in life.

Loneliness should first and foremost draw you to God. He loves you. He wants to spend time with you. He wants to be your everything. He might not take away your loneliness that stems from your singleness. But you better believe he wants to walk through that loneliness right by your side, drawing you closer to himself through it all.

Loneliness can be one of the greatest blessings we can ever have because it can drive us to pursue our greatest need – a personal relationship with the Father, Son, and Holy Spirit. Dwell on Bible verses like these.

> "The LORD is near to the brokenhearted and saves the crushed in spirit." (Psalm 34:18)

> "Fear not, for I am with you; be not dismayed, for I am your God; I will strengthen you, I will help you, I will uphold you with my righteous right hand." (Isaiah 41:10)

> "Even though I walk through the valley of the shadow of death, I will fear no evil, for you are with me; your rod and your staff, they comfort me." (Psalm 23:4)

> "Be strong and courageous. Do not fear or be in dread of them, for it is the Lord your God who goes with you. He will not leave you or forsake you." (Deuteronomy 31:6)

> "Do not be anxious about anything, but in everything by prayer and supplication with thanksgiving let your requests be made known to God. And the peace of God, which surpasses all understanding, will guard your hearts and your minds in Christ Jesus." (Philippians 4:6-7)

It's one thing to read and memorize Bible verses like these, but your loneliness has given you an opportunity to experience God's closeness. Don't waist that opportunity.

Loneliness is a real struggle for many Christians who are in a season of singleness. Don't be ashamed. But also don't respond to your loneliness in sinful ways. You are not alone. Seek healthy relationships, and above all seek Christ.

# Study Questions

1. Before reading this chapter, how did you feel about your loneliness? Guilty, ashamed, annoyed, denial? After reading this chapter, has anything changed?

2. Which of the five points do you feel like you can do a better job at? If none of them resonated with you, what do you think you need to do to respond in a healthy way to feelings of loneliness?

3. During your season of singleness, why are other people (meaning people who are not romantic possibilities) so important to your spiritual, mental, emotional, and overall health?

# Chapter 10

# Sexual Purity: How the Church Often Gets It Wrong

The American Church has gotten the issue of sexual purity backwards. The idea is presented to youth groups across the country that it is utterly crucial for them to "remain pure." When they are virgins, they have their purity. If they have premarital sex, however, they will lose their purity.

### True Purity Is Given By Jesus Christ Alone

While there are certainly worse things you could tell a teenager, this logic simply does not translate to our spiritual reality explained in the Bible. We most certainly should teach abstinence, but the motivation behind abstinence is often neglected.

The Bible explains that if you truly are pure, then your actions will be pure. The fact that people "lose their purity" shows that they were never truly and spiritually pure to begin with. Our actions are a reflection of who we are and what we believe. A good tree produces good fruit, and a bad tree produces bad fruit (Matthew 7:17). Likewise, a pure tree produces pure fruit and an impure tree produces impure fruit.

Since we were all born impure (Psalm 51:5), purity is not something to be lost. Purity is something that can only be given to us through Jesus Christ (1 Corinthians 1:30 NLT). In the highest sense possible, you can't lose your purity because you were never truly pure to begin with. If you were pure you would never have done those sexually impure things. The fruit reflects the tree.

**If You Think You Are Pure Because You're Young, You Will Feel More Shame the Older You Get**

This is one of the biggest lies the American church has fed our young people, specifically our young ladies. Telling them they have a purity they can lose is not only unhelpful in keeping young people from sexual sin, it also only magnifies their shame when they do sin sexually.

We should definitely teach our young people to abstain from sexual sin, but we should explain that they should do so because they are seeking to honor Christ as they live from the purity he has given them through his gospel, not so they can earn their own purity through their works (or lack of external sexual sin).

We should warn young Christians (and all Christians) of the consequences of sexual sin, but we should also warn them of the consequences of thinking they are pure without Christ. There are countless benefits that we will reap if we avoid external sexual sins. We must preach abstinence for the unmarried as this is biblical and right. But there are also countless consequences we will reap if we think we can earn our purity through abstinence rather than receive it through the gospel of Jesus Christ (Ephesians 2:8-10).

When the Church only teaches Christians to keep something they never had to begin with, they are doomed to fail. Purity is given by Christ. You can't walk in something you never really had.

The idea that you are born pure and then you can lose your purity is also dangerous because those who do not struggle with sexual sin as much as others believe they really do have a purity of their own. Ironically, people who think they are pure because they haven't engaged in sexual impurity are probably the least pure of them all because they are most likely relying on their own works rather than on God's grace. In Jesus' warning to the Pharisees he explained this point further:

> "First clean the inside of the cup and the plate, that the outside also may be clean. Woe to you, scribes and Pharisees, hypocrites! For you are like whitewashed tombs, which outwardly appear beautiful, but within are full of dead people's bones and all uncleanness. So you also outwardly appear righteous to others, but within you are full of hypocrisy and lawlessness" (Matthew 23:26-28)

We must apply this truth to our sexuality. We must seek the purity only Christ can give on the inside so that our external actions will also be clean.

Even if you believe that you are pure because you don't engage in sexual sin, internally you will know you are not what you are pretending to be. I have witnessed firsthand how prevalent this is among young women who have grown up in the church. They get exalted because of their abstinence, but internally they feel ashamed and guilty because they know they are not as pure as people think they are.

## The Resurrection of Jesus Christ Transfers His Purity to Us

One of my favorite Bible verses about our new life in Christ is Romans 6:4, "We were therefore buried with him through baptism into death in order that, just as Christ was raised from the dead through the glory of the Father, we too may live a new life."

The Greek words used in Romans 6:4 that are translated "new life" are "kainotes" for "new" and "zoe" for "life." Kainotes means "newness of spirit." This is not the type of "new" like when I get a new pair of shoes, which in a year from now will no longer be new. This word denotes that the whole substance is now different. What you were is no longer even the same material as what you are now. Kainotes is that which replaces the obsolete with something that is better, superior, or more advanced.

For example, compared to the typewriter the computer is a new way to print words. Email is a new form of sending information compared to mailing a letter through the post office. Kainotes means different in substance, not chronological order. The computer has been around for a while now, so it's not new in that sense, but compared to the typewriter, it's different, better, and new.

For the word "life" Paul used the Greek word "zoe" rather than the word "bios." Bios refers to the type of life that is observable on the outside which you can record. It's where we get our English word for "biography." Zoe however refers to a metaphysical life, a life force that animates a living being.

Therefore "new life" in Romans 6:4, "kainotes zoe," does not mean a fresh start, a new chapter in your biography, or a second chance. It means you have a new name written in an entirely different book. You are not a better version of the former you. You are now a totally new and different person. You have a new heart and a new spirit. You're of a different substance now, unrelated to your sinful nature. Martin Loyd Jones, teaching on Romans 6, helps us apply this theological knowledge in a practical way:

"Paul never says that sin is dead; what he does say is that we are dead to sin. Sin is still alive in our mortal body; and if we do not realize that and deal with it, it will soon reign in our mortal body. Sin is not eradicated out of us, and it never will be as long as we are in this mortal body. Sin is in our mortal body and it is always striving for mastery and for control in the Christian. It can never dominate over the life of Christ in him, but it is always striving to dominate his body. It may indeed dominate his body for a time, and when it does so, it is what we call "backsliding." Sin is there . . . you always have to remember that, and not allow it [to take control]."

So what does this mean in relation to sexual temptation? It means your porn problem is not a computer problem. Could you imagine buying a computer, and then trying to return it the next day, "So, what's wrong with this computer that you want to return?" the salesman asks. "Well," you respond, "this one seems to be malfunctioning. It keeps causing me to lust over things I shouldn't?"

If we hope to overcome sexual temptation, we must not only believe that our old self is dead to us, but we must also believe that we are new in Christ. We reject the old desires while simultaneously embracing the new desires. When lust is lurking, you have to remember who you really are. You desire purity, you desire to please God, and you desire to live free. You now desire what is good because Christ has raised you from the dead and made you good.

# Study Questions

1. What were you taught about sexual purity? How has this negatively or positively affected your life?

2. Why is it important to deal with our sexuality during our season of singleness? If you feel guilty or prideful about your purity, what should you do?

3. How does the cross and resurrection of Jesus Christ impact our purity?

*(Note: Much of the material from this chapter was taken from my book, Redeemed Like David: How to Overcome Sexual Temptation.)*

# Chapter 11

# What Christian Singles Should Know About Homosexuality

If you are a Christian single with homosexual urges, you are getting pulled in so many different directions these days. Is it okay to be a homosexual Christian? Can you practice homosexuality if you are a Christian? Or should you just practice abstinence completely?

These are tough questions you will have to weigh through. I wish we had more time in this book to study these questions, but unfortunately we don't. What I would like to do is just touch on the basics.

Perhaps you are a Christian single who has never struggled with homosexual tendencies. Either way, you live in a society where you as a Christian will be forced to comment and dialogue about this topic. So it will be beneficial for us all to review one of the most basic questions people ask about homosexuality, which is whether or not it is a choice.

So does the Bible say being gay is a choice? All sin is a choice. Therefore, one way to answer "Does the Bible say being gay is a choice?" is to decide if being gay is a sin according to the Bible.

## The Bible Does Say Being Gay Is a Choice Because All Sin Is Choice

To clarify, by the term "being gay," I mean those who are practicing homosexuals. This does not refer to those who are tempted in gay ways and yet are resisting the temptation in order to obey God. "Being gay" means you are living an actively gay life.

1 Corinthians 6:9-10 states, "Or do you not know that the unrighteous will not inherit the kingdom of God? Do not be deceived: neither the sexually immoral, nor idolaters, nor adulterers, nor men who practice homosexuality, nor thieves, nor the greedy, nor drunkards, nor revilers, nor swindlers will inherit the kingdom of God."

Since all sin is a choice, and practicing homosexuality is a sin, it is safe to conclude that the Bible does say being gay is a choice.

### The Bible Does Say Being Gay Is a Choice Because We All Choose to Obey Our Sinful Nature

Despite what many believe and proclaim, there is not a consensus among the scientific community on the relationship between being gay and human genes. However, let's assume there is a connection between being gay and the genes a person is born with.

Even if you had a natural, genetic disposition towards being gay, the Bible says "practicing homosexuality" is still your personal choice. The Bible says that everyone is born sinful (Psalm 51:5, Romans 5:12). The Bible refers to this as original sin. All of our bodies, because of our inherited sinful nature, have certain sinful tendencies. And yet the Bible also states that all sin is still our own personal choice:

> "None is righteous, no, not one; no one understands; no one seeks for God. All have turned aside; together they have become worthless; no one does good, not even one." (Romans 3:10-12)

"…for all have sinned and fall short of the glory of God." (Romans 3:23)

We "all have sinned" means we have all chosen to sin. Again, the Bible states that we are all born sinful *and* we all choose to sin. Therefore, even if you were born with gay tendencies, the Bible would still say that you have the choice to "practice homosexuality."

**What's Truly Behind the Question, "Does the Bible Say Being Gay Is a Choice?"**

"Does the Bible say being gay is a choice?" is a hand grenade question in our current American society. It was front page news when 2016 presidential candidate Dr. Ben Carson was asked by a female LGBT activist, "Do you think it was my choice to be gay?" Since Dr. Carson has gotten into trouble in the past for stating that he does believe being gay is a choice, he gave the young lady a polite political response, "It's a long answer to that question." Seeing that Dr. Carson was not going to engage her, she walked away, but not before looking him in the eyes and angrily stating, "I think you're full of %#*#."

The LBGT activist's reaction to Dr. Ben Carson's answer shows there is often a deeper motive behind the question, "Does the Bible say being gay is a choice?" To reveal that motive, perhaps it would help to ask another question, "Is choosing to be gay a bad choice?"

Why do people care so much if being gay is a choice or not? People care if being gay is a choice because people know practicing homosexuality is wrong. Even people who do not believe the Bible still have some form of a moral compass since they are made in the image of God, though this compass is clearly not fully accurate since our image bearing of God is so broken. Theologically this is referred to as the "moral law."

The moral law states that within humans there is a general understanding of right and wrong. For example: no matter where you go, whether you are in New York City or you are with a tribe in the heart of Uganda, everyone knows stealing is wrong. Everywhere on earth, at all times in human history, stealing has always been a punishable crime. Why? Because the moral law is written on the human heart (Romans 2:14-16).

The point is this: if being gay was a good choice, then people would not be so passionate about the question, "Is being gay a choice?" If they feel it's completely right to be gay, then why is it not celebrated that people make their own choice to be gay? Why do people get angry when you say being gay is a choice? Answer: Deep down they already know being gay is a sin because of the moral law written on their hearts, even if they would never admit this. And one of their best ways of coping with that nagging feeling that their doing something wrong is to justify it by saying it's not their choice.

It's much like our court systems today. If you can prove the criminal has a "disease" or "disorder" or is "insane," the crime is less punishable, and in some cases not punishable at all. Since people know practicing gayness is a sin, they try to escape this reality by stating they are born with it. And yet within this argument, those justifying homosexuality are treating it like it's some sort of bad disease you are born with. Why? Because deep down they know homosexuality is a sin, a crime in the eyes of God, which will be judged along with all other sins in God's court.

People don't argue about having genes that make them want to serve the poor because this is a good choice. People celebrate good choices. People like to take credit for good choices. People not wanting to take credit for being gay proves these people know it is a wrong choice.

## Sometimes You Should Not Answer the Questions, "Does the Bible Say Being Gay Is a Choice?" Without First Asking Your Own Question

As exemplified through Dr. Ben Carson's experience with the LGBT activist, some people are not asking "Does the Bible say being gay is a choice?" with ears to really hear your answer.

The Bible says that when this happens, you should not waste your time (Matthew 7:6, 2 Timothy 2:23). When you are asked a question that has hidden motives meant to trap you, do what Jesus did:

> "And they came again to Jerusalem. And as he was walking in the temple, the chief priests and the scribes and the elders came to him, and they said to him, "By what authority are you doing these things, or who gave you this authority to do them?" Jesus said to them, "I will ask you one question; answer me, and I will tell you by what authority I do these things. Was the baptism of John from heaven or from man? Answer me." And they discussed it with one another, saying, "If we say, 'From heaven,' he will say, 'Why then did you not believe him?' But shall we say, 'From man'?"— they were afraid of the people, for they all held that John really was a prophet. So they answered Jesus, "We do not know." And Jesus said to them, "Neither will I tell you by what authority I do these things." (Mark 11:27-33)

They tried to trap Jesus. They wanted him to say he was the Son of God so they could crucify him. And if he said he was not the Son of God, well then they won there too. Jesus is the Son of God, a fact he proclaimed often, but rather than play into their hands, he asked them his own trapping question.

The same can be done when someone asks about what the Bible says regarding homosexuality. Of course, if they truly want to know, you should do your best to explain the biblical truth. However, if they are only asking this so they can crucify you, then perhaps the best response is to ask a question of your own, "Do you think being gay is a good choice?" If they answer yes, then you can respond, "Then why don't you take credit for making that good choice?" And if they answer that being gay is a bad choice, well then perhaps they are ready to hear the gospel of Jesus Christ.

## Don't Bash Yourself or Other People With Biblical Truth. Choose Love Every Time

So does the Bible say being gay is a choice? The Bible says all sin is a choice, including the choice to practice homosexuality. And the Bible also says that all sin can be washed away through the gospel of Jesus Christ (John 3:16, 1 John 1:8-10). May we Christians not argue with people who just want to argue. May we, instead, seek to share the gospel whenever an opportunity presents itself.

If you struggle with homosexuality, I want you to know all Christians struggle with sin. I'm sorry our society and the church have made you feel your sin is worse than everyone else's sin. It's not. We all sin. But I also want to love you by telling you the truth: there is no excuse to sin.

God always provides a way out, even from homosexuality, "No temptation has overtaken you that is not common to man. God is faithful, and he will not let you be tempted beyond your ability, but with the temptation he will also provide the way of escape, that you may be able to endure it" (1 Corinthians 10:13). Seek Christ in the midst of your struggle with homosexuality. He's allowed this to take place in your life for the same reasons he allows every trial and temptation in all of our lives – to draw you closer to him.

Perhaps God will set you free and allow you to regain a desire for the opposite sex. Or perhaps God will give you the strength to live a life of abstinence. Either way, I know God wants you to love and seek him above everything and everyone else.

If you don't struggle with homosexuality, try to be sensitive, kind, and loving towards those who do. Don't act like their sin is not sin, but also don't judge them for their sin or act as though their sin is worse than yours. Love them. Walk with God. Ask him to show you what to say and what not to say. Ask him to help you to love all people with your deeds first, only offering words once someone knows you truly have their best interest at heart.

# Study Questions

1. Whether you struggle with homosexual tendencies or not, why is it important for all Christians to know what the Bible says about this topic? What do you think the Bible says about homosexuality and gay marriage?

2. If someone is a Christian single and struggles with homosexuality, what should they do?

3. How can the church and individual Christians love Christian singles who struggle with homosexuality?

# Chapter 12

## 4 Christ-Centered Ways to Change Things About Yourself That Need to Be Changed

As you've read through this book or just spent honest times of reflection in God's presence and in his word, surely you've become aware of things about yourself you wish you could change. When it comes to our study of singleness, there may even be things about yourself that are hindering you from finding a future spouse (or from enjoying your life of singleness).

Everyone has something in their life they want to change. Whether it's a New Year's resolution, an addictive sin pattern, or just an annoying habit you are finally fed up with, the Bible states that change is possible. But it's not easy. And certain changes can only be done through the power of Jesus Christ.

Therefore, here are four Christ-centered ways to change your life.

### Change Your Identity Through Christ to Change Your Life

The primary Christian way to change your life is to change your identity through the grace of Jesus Christ. At the core of Christian doctrine is the idea that who you are will determine what you will do. The world opposes this idea and states that to change yourself, you just need to change your actions. But again, Christianity states that to change your actions, your identity needs to change first. Jesus explains it this ways:

> "For no good tree bears bad fruit, nor again does a bad tree bear good fruit, for each tree is known by its own

> fruit. For figs are not gathered from thorn bushes, nor are grapes picked from a bramble bush. The good person out of the good treasure of his heart produces good, and the evil person out of his evil treasure produces evil, for out of the abundance of the heart his mouth speaks." (Luke 6:43-45)

The Christian way to change your life is to change your very identity as a person through putting your faith (active trust) in Jesus Christ. When we believe Jesus is Lord, ask him to be our Lord, follow him as our Lord, and rely on him to transfer his righteousness to us rather than relying on our own good works, the Bible explains that we are transformed into a new creation (2 Corinthians 5:17). We are born again when we believe in Jesus Christ as our Savior (John 3:3, 16).

## Change Your Beliefs About Your Identity in Christ to Change Your Life

After your identity has truly been changed when you become a Christian, the next most important change that must occur is your belief about your identity. The Christian way to change your life starts with a change in identity, but to carry this change through into action, we must also change what we believe about our self and about our desires.

Justification is an act done to us at the moment of our conversions. Justification means God transferred the holiness, perfections, and guiltlessness of Christ completely onto us. When God looks at us, he sees us with the purity of Christ. Sanctification, however, is the process by which we learn to actually put into action the justification that is completely ours in Christ. We are totally holy in Christ, but our life is not totally holy in our behaviors.

Hebrews 10:14 explains, "For by a single offering he has perfected for all time those who are being sanctified." In the NIV, it states we are made perfect for all time as we are being "made holy." So yes, Christ has made us perfect forever through his one sacrifice. But we are also in the process of being made holy through sanctification.

Our sanctification will grow the more deeply we believe in our justification through Christ. Sin occurs when we believe we want a pleasure outside of God's will. To change your life and behavior, you must change your beliefs about what you really want and about who you really are. Christians do not believe in something that's not true. Our justification in Christ is real, and the more deeply we believe this, the more it will show in our sanctification.

If you desire to change your eating habits, you must believe that since you are a new creation in Christ, you desire to eat in a righteous way, even when you feel like you want to eat in an unrighteous way. If you desire to change your sexual sin patters, you must first believe that you are no longer a person who finds pleasure in sexual sin, but now you are a child of God who finds pleasure in obeying your Heavenly Father.

The Christian way to change your life is to change what you believe about your identity and desires.

**Change Who Influences You to Change Your Life**

One of the most significant Christian ways to change your life is to change the community you live in. I don't mean the physical location of your house, but rather the social circles with which you spend the majority of your time. As the saying goes, "Show me your friends and I'll show you your future."

We might think we are the exception to the rule, but no matter who we are, the people we choose to spend our time with will have a direct influence on our life and behavior patterns.

Proverbs 13:20 says, "Whoever walks with the wise becomes wise, but the companion of fools will suffer harm." Paul states in 1 Corinthians 15:33, "Do not be deceived: 'Bad company ruins good morals.'" Paul tells us "do not be deceived" because we all are tempted to deceive ourselves by thinking that we can keep unhealthy people in our lives and yet remain healthy ourselves. While we certainly can't cut off everyone who is imperfect (because we all our imperfect), and while we should have people in our lives we are trying to help, we must also make sure we have a core community that is seeking to live a Christ-like life just as we desire to live.

This is why the Christian way to change your life must involve the church. I don't mean a building but the body of Christ. There's no such thing as a solo Christian in the Bible. We are all one in Christ (Galatians 3:28). We are all a part of the universal church whether we like it or not, and we all should be a part of the local church. We need to help one another and be helped by one another. To be detached from other Christians is to be detached from the body of Christ (1 Corinthians 12:27).

**Change Your Life Through Christ Alone**

The above Christian ways to change your life are just a small sample of the many ways the Bible teaches us on how to change. Of course we must also regularly pray and take the Bible into our hearts, we must read good Christian books, and we must live a life of serving others.

But above all, we must remember that Jesus Christ alone is our hope.

To change our identity, we need Christ. To change our beliefs, we need Christ. To change our circle of influence, we need Christ. To become the best Christian man or woman you can be, you need Christ. Above all, the Christian way to change your life is through Christ alone.

> "I am the vine; you are the branches. Whoever abides in me and I in him, he it is that bears much fruit, for apart from me you can do nothing." (John 15:5)

We will never be able to change our life and behavior without the active power of Jesus.

## Study Questions

1. What have you tried to change about yourself before and how did you try to change? How did it go?

2. Summarize your answer to this question, "How can a Christian change their behavior?" (Many say, "You can't change. Christ has to do it for you." Yes, Christ is the only way to change. But throughout the Bible, God commands people to actively participate in the sanctification process (2 Peter 1:5). So to ask it another way, "How can a Christian participate in the sanctification process?")

3. What might you need to change about yourself to enhance your joy in Christ during your season of singleness and to move on from your season of singleness (if you desire to be married)? How are planning to make this change?

# Section 3:

# Preparing Your Heart for Your Future

# Chapter 13

# What Is God's Purpose for You?

Throughout our whole lives, we all will constantly come back to this questions, "What is my purpose?" During our years of singleness, however, when so much of lives is still unsettled and unknown, this is perhaps the most asked question of all. To answer this question, perhaps it would help to ask a few more questions.

Why do most of us want our specific calling to be very flashy and important? Why do people want to be at the center of the story, to be famous, to have more followers on their social media platforms? Why is there even a need for words like "selfies"? Even the recluse is often a loner not because he hates the attention of people but because he wants it so bad it has paralyzed him, making him so fearful of rejection he would rather avoid everyone all together.

The Christian knows in her spirit this desire is wrong, even if she doesn't know why it is wrong. Aside from the fact that there are plane verses all over the Bible condemning all forms of idolatry, including the idolatry of people, I think there is one main reason the Christian feels the guilt of self-exaltation. It has to do with our purpose and God's glory.

### Our Purpose Is to Glorify God

Everything God does, he ultimately does for his name's sake, for his glory (Psalm 19:1-4, Psalm 23:3, Ezekiel 20:9, Ezekiel 36:22-32, John 8:50, John 12:27-28,John 17:1, Romans 1:5, Romans 11:36, 1 Corinthians 10:31, Colossians 1:15-20). Our purpose, therefore, is to glorify God.

But what is God's glory? When you see some invisible quality of God in a visible (or knowable) way, it's called "the glory of God." That's why, for example, when God would reveal himself in the Old Testament to the Israelites in a cloud or in fire it says the "glory of God" would appear (Exodus 24:15-18).

In Isaiah 6:3 the angels are singing, "Holy, holy, holy is the LORD Almighty; the whole earth is full of his glory." You would expect the text to read that the whole earth is full of his holiness; but when the attributes of God become visible, in this case his holiness, the Bible calls it glory.

When Moses asked to see God's glory, God responded by saying, "I will make all my goodness pass before you and will proclaim before you my name 'The LORD' (Exodus 33:19). God showed Moses his glory, therefore he showed Moses all his goodness and made his name known to Moses. God made his qualities visible and knowable to Moses because this was the same thing as showing Moses' his glory.

So when we say that our purpose is to glorify God, it means we are to bear God's image and make God known to the world.

## If Our Purpose Is to Glorify God, Then Our Purpose Is to Reflect Jesus

Jesus glorifies God the most because he makes the invisible qualities of God visible better than anyone else ever could. Colossians 1:15 states, "The Son is the image of the invisible God," and Hebrews 1:3 explains, "The Son is the radiance of God's glory and the exact representation of his being, sustaining all things by his powerful word." John 1:14, 18 (ESV) adds that "And the Word became flesh and dwelt among us, and we have seen his glory, glory as of the only Son from the Father, full of grace and truth. . . . No one has ever seen God; the only God, who is at the Father's side, he has made him known."

What does all this mean? It means that what we know about God is what we can see in the face of Jesus (2 Corinthians 4:4, 6).

God's writing this story we are all living in so he as the opportunity to express himself to the people he loves, and in expressing himself he is bringing himself glory, making the invisible visible. God made us with the same purpose. He made us for his glory (Isaiah 43:7), therefore he made us in his image (Genesis 1:27). Since Jesus reveals the most about God and thus glorifies God most, our purpose is to bear the image of Christ (Romans 8:29).

The problem occurred when we veered from God's plan.

## Sin Is the Opposite of Our Purpose Because It's the Opposite of Glorifying God

The literal translation of the word "sin" means to "miss the mark" and was used to describe an arrow missing the intended target. To understand how we miss the mark, we must first know what we were supposed to be aiming at.

Sin is breaking God's commands. But God's commands are not a random lists of do's-and-do-not's as though God could have reversed all the ten commandments and then those would have been the law (e.g. thought shall murder, though shall commit adultery, etc.).

God's law, like everything in its original form, is an expression of who God is. The law was meant to make the invisible character of God visible to us. God commands us not to murder because he is just. He commands us to have one wife because he is faithful. He commands us not to steal because he is honest. He commands us to be holy, "for it is written, 'Be holy, because I am holy'" (1 Peter 1:16). All the commandments of God are an extension of the very character of God. Therefore, to break God's commands is to conceal God's expression of himself, to cast a shadow on his image (glory).

Romans 3:23 explains, "for all have sinned and fall short of the glory of God." You'd think it would say that all have sinned and broken God's commands, but to break God's commands is to fall short of hitting the mark of reflecting God properly. To obey God's commands is to fulfill God's purpose because it is to bear his image, reflect his nature, and thus glorify him by making his invisible qualities visible through actions which reflect God's character.

You know who is Lord of your life by who you are seeking to bring praise. If you are mainly seeking personal glorification (visibility), then you are seeking to live as your own god, as the main character in the story.

## Our Purpose Is to Glorify God Through His Grace

To right what went wrong, we must seek the transforming grace of God so we will be able to once again play the original purpose God made for us in his story. And it is his story we are living in, whether we choose to believe this or not.

God is at the center, the sun is symbolizing him, we are caught in his orbit, reflecting his rays. Our purpose is to glorify God, to bear his image, and reveal the truth about him to the watching world. Since Jesus is the exact visible representation of God because he is God (Hebrews 1:3), our goal must be to walk as Jesus did (1 John 2:6).

Romans 8:28-29, "And we know that for those who love God all things work together for good, for those who are called according to his purpose. For those whom he foreknew he also predestined to be conformed to the image of his Son . . . ." God has a purpose for us all, and that purpose is to make us look and act like his Son, so we might glorify God. The more we look and act like Jesus, the more we will reveal God to the world, making the invisible visible, thus glorifying our Lord. And the only way we will look like Jesus is through the gospel.

God's ultimate plan is to bring glory to himself, thus our purpose, in union with the Spirit, is to reveal God by reflecting Jesus through his transforming grace.

## Study Questions

1. What is the glory of God? What does it mean to say, "Our purpose is to glorify God?"

2. What is sin? Why does sin not glorify God?

3. How can you glorify God during your season of singleness?

# Chapter 14

# How to Figure Out God's Plan for You (Desire Reveals Design)

How do I figure out God's plan for me? What does God want me to do with my life? How do I know God's purpose for me? What's God's calling on me? How can I know God's will for my life? How do I know if God is leading me down this path or that? God, please help me figure out your plan for me!

It can be confusing to know what God has called us to do, especially during your years of singleness when so many questions about your future are still unanswered. One way to figure out God's plan for you is to look at what you have a longing to do.

**Holy Desires Reveal a Holy Design**

While not every desire will come to fruition, and certainly not come to fruition the way we thought it would, it still brings wonderful direction to our lives when we look at what good desires God has placed in our hearts. (Notice the emphasis on "good" desires. Of course this should not include sinful desires. When we follow God, our desires will change and we will desire to be what he wants.)

None of this means that our calling will always correspond to our desire for ease and smooth sailing towards our ideal vision of life for ourselves. Just because you have to do things you don't like is no reason to assume that you are missing God's will for your life. God will have us do things we don't like.

When trying to figure out God's plan for your life, expect there to be long periods of hard training.

## God's Sovereignty Does Not Cancel Our Need for Personal Effort and Training

God's foreordination does not contradict our need to put forth hard work to become what he has planned. The fact that God has a real plan for life just means that we will be miserable if we try to reject that plan. By rejecting rather than embracing the will of God for your life, you will achieve neither what you want nor what God wants for you.

True happiness is found when we work hard to become who God has preplanned for us to be (Ephesians 2:10, Philippians 3:12-16). Like Paul who used to persecute believers of the gospel only to then be transformed, Paul's desire drastically changed when he followed Christ, "Woe to me if I do not preach the gospel!" (1 Corinthians 9:16).

1 Corinthians 9:16 shows not only how Paul's desire drastically changed, but how miserable he would be if he were to reject God's plan for him. Likewise, if we do not do what he calls us to, we will eventually have to cry out "Woe to me." God's specific design for us is revealed through our specific desires in us. Just as Paul's desperate desire to preach revealed his calling and gifting to preach, we too should seek to do what we cannot do without.

## God Will Sanctify Our Desires Throughout Our Lives

To balance all this, we must be humble enough to know that some of the desires we have are not yet fully sanctified and developed in us by God, therefore we should not expect to know our whole life plan at the age of 25.

We must be realistic enough to know that who we are now is not who we will always be as we continue to grow and mature. We must expect some of our desires to not be fulfilled the way we originally hoped, or in some cases not at all.

God has a good plan for our lives. Therefore, life should not be a journey in seeking to be what we think we want. Rather, we should seek God above all, and then see what he makes us into. When we seek to obey and please God, we need not worry that our life will be miserable, fearing God has planned something for us which we will not desire. For when we seek God, our plans will change through the course of our lives, but so will our desires.

When Paul was Saul, he could never have guessed his ultimate desire would be to preach the gospel he was persecuting. But when Saul was transformed by the grace of God into the Paul who loves Christ, Paul's desires changed too. The same will be true of us. The more deeply we come to love God and are sanctified in him, the more our desires will be conformed to the plans God has always had for us.

So when you are following and obeying God, a good way to figure out what God has planned for you to do is to look at what you desire to do.

# Study Questions

1. Read 1 Peter 4:7-11. Why is it important to know what gifts God has blessed you with? What should you do with those gifts?

2. How can our desires help us know what we might be called to do?

3. How and why will our desires change throughout our lives?

# Chapter 15

# 2 Questions to Ask If You Want to Know What Your Specific Calling Is from God

Every Christian wants to know what their calling is from God. However, this question is perhaps one of the most difficult to answer for a variety of reasons: you have to know you are actually hearing from God, you have to know the Scriptures to make sure your calling is congruent with truth, you have to be flexible enough to know who you are today is not who God will make you into five years from now, and you have to be humble enough to accept that your understanding of God's calling on you will progress and even change throughout the years.

So how do we know what our calling is from God? It helps to break this questions up into two parts: 1. What always is your ultimate calling? 2. What is your specific calling in this season of life?

## What Is Your Ultimate Calling from God?

Question one is rather simple to answer biblically (see chapter 13). Every Christian's ultimate calling is to love God, obey God, please God, serve God – in short, glorifying God is your ultimate calling. Wherever you are at in life, whatever skills you currently possess, whatever opportunities are available to you, glorifying God is your purpose.

The confusion sets in when we begin to seek how to accomplish this ultimate calling from God in specific and individual ways. Each Christian has a spiritual gift, and some of us have the same spiritual gifts as each other. But none of us are the same person. We all have different personalities. Christian ministry is simply expressing God's spiritual gifts in individual, personal ways.

I may have the spiritual gift of teaching, but the way I express this gift in writing will be different than how you may express this gift through a video podcast or preaching. My mom may have the gift of hospitality and expresses this gift through hosting borders at her house. You may also have the gift of hospitality, but you might never consider letting someone live in your house for an extended period of time. Nick may have the spiritual gift of administration expressed in his ability to organize teams of people, but you may have the gift of administration while not being able to stand working with volunteers.

So how do we know how we should individually express our spiritual gifts? How do we know what our current, specific calling is from God?

## Your Calling from God Will Be a Passion of Yours and Profitable to Others

Doing what you enjoy without helping other people is a hobby. Helping other people without doing what you personally enjoy is just a job. Your God given calling intersects at the place where your passion and other people's profitability meet.

To have a powerful, impactful, and sustainable ministry, you have to find the place where your desire satisfies a real need in the world. If all you do is think about what you like to do and in the process no one is helped but you, that is not a real calling from God. If, however, you are benefiting a lot of people but you are miserable in the process, that too is not a calling from God.

While it's good soul care, it's not healthy to go on a hike by yourself and think this is your calling from God. It's good self-care to paint a picture that will only be displayed in your house. It's biblical to enjoy the company of friends to simply enjoy them. But if our joy terminates on us and doesn't benefit others we have not found our Christ-centered calling.

It's also necessary at times to fulfill service roles that don't exactly give you the best opportunity to express your specific gifts and passions. Sometimes a disaster hits and you just need to roll up your sleeves and serve people, even if your best skill is to organize or teach or offer wisdom or give money generously. If there's rubble in the streets trapping people, you need to go pick up that rubble even if you don't like physical labor.

With all that said, if you just do a ministry that is helpful to others but you're not that equipped to do it, eventually you will get burned out. And if you just sit alone doing some hobby you personally enjoy, eventually you will feel so purposeless and useless the hobby will become a curse.

The place where God is calling you is the place where your passion and productivity meet. If you enjoy doing something and when you do it you produce good fruit for God that actually benefits people, odds are that is a your current calling from God.

Paul proclaimed, "Woe to me if I do not preach the gospel!" (1 Corinthians 9:16). His passion was preaching. People benefited from his preaching. Thus it was clear preaching was his calling.

## Your Calling from God Is Always Fruitful, Not Always Financially Successful

It's great when you can be paid to do your passion in life. But just because you are not getting paid to do what you love does not mean it can't be your current calling from God. Likewise, just because you can do certain things so well that people are willing to pay you, this is not a guarantee that God is calling you to continue in this endeavor.

Careers are good. It's good to make money. Sometimes God blesses you with a career that is totally unrelated to your calling, passion, or spiritual gift from God. Later in life you might discover you have a heart for pastoring people, but early in life God may have led you to become an accountant. This scenario does not mean you missed God's calling for your life even though you want to be a pastor but now you are stuck without a seminary degree, you have a family to support, and you can't do what you need to do to become an ordained minister.

Even if you never are paid to be a pastor, you can still keep your job as an accountant and fulfill your calling from God. You can express your pastoral gift without having the office or title of pastor. You don't need to be an official pastor to express your pastoral gifting. There is no limit to the examples of how you can use your pastor-gift to help other people: counseling a friend, leading your children, facilitating a small group Bible study, teaching a class, mentoring some younger men.

You can apply the above example to whatever it is you have a passion for. Don't let your lack of a paycheck be an excuse to not fulfill and enjoy your calling from God.

## You Will Know Your Calling from God When Other People Know It Too

If no one on planet earth thinks your gift is teaching, then you probably don't have the gift of teaching. If no one would ever ask you for advice, you are probably not equipped to be a counselor. If you are the last person someone would come to when they are in a financial pinch, your probably don't have the gift of generosity.

God has placed each individual Christian in the midst of the church, which is the collective group of Christians. The natural and normal way for people to know their calling from God is for it to be confirmed through multiple other Christians. Your gift will be recognized by others when they are benefitted by it or when they see it powerfully expressed in your life. In short, you can't be the only person to know what your true gift from God really is (1 Timothy 4:14-16).

## How to Know What Your Calling Is from God

Certainly there are many more ways to know what your calling is from God. Knowing your calling, however, starts with knowing what your gifts are. You then have to discover what passion you have for expressing these gifts. Lastly, you must make sure other Christians can confirm the fruitfulness of your life when you walk in your calling.

These are just a few biblical ways you can know what your calling is from God. Ultimately, you have to read the word of God, pray, and trust that the Lord will reveal and confirm what his specific calling on your life is right now.

# Study Questions

1. What's the difference between your ultimate calling and your specific calling?

2. What balance should there be between personal enjoyment and helping other people with real needs they have?

3. Why is it important that other people within the church also know what your gifts are?

# Chapter 16

# 4 Tips to Help You Recover From Past Breakups

Dating breakups are common. Most 20-to-30-somethings have been in multiple dating relationships. Not all breakups are because of sin. Maybe after time, the two of you just realized it wasn't meant to be. Or perhaps some of those relationships were sinful and ended because God wasn't in it.

Regardless of the reason for the breakup, the weeks and months that follow can feel like you just got shoved down a river without a rafting guide and now you need to figure out how to survive class V whitewater rapids on the fly.

Jesus doesn't want that for you. While the Bible doesn't talk about dating breakups, it does talk a lot about forgiveness, healing, and living a healthy life for God's glory. So here are four quick biblical tips that will help prepare you for the future by helping you deal with any past breakups that were unhealthy.

## #1: Don't Form Unbiblical Beliefs in Response to Your Breakup

As A.W. Tozer said, "What comes into our minds when we think about God is the most important thing about us." Satan knows this is true, therefore he uses every opportunity to try and twist our understanding of God's truth.

"Does God really love me?" "Does God have a good plan for my life?" "Maybe I'll never find a spouse if I only date Christians." "I've tried to follow God's laws and where has that got me? I'm done with this!"

None of us would accept statements like these in a right state of mind. But after a breakup, you are vulnerable. Just as Satan waited until Jesus was hungry, temptations to believe the worst about God come at us when we are at our weakest (Luke 4:2).

Be on guard after a breakup. Trust your Bible more than your emotions. If you realize you've started to believe lies about God's love for you because of a bad breakup, renounce those lies, repent, and actively believe God's word.

## #2: Don't Skip the Grieving Process, But Don't Cling to It Either

To heal properly, you have to embrace the reality of your loss. If you never allow yourself to accept that you were hurt after the breakup, you will slow the healing process, or even miss it altogether.

To recover after a dating relationship ends, you need to allow yourself a healthy emotional grieving time. A good rule of thumb is that the longer the relationship was, the longer the time of grieving should be. I won't put an actual time frame on it. Pray about it. God will make it clear. Think in terms of weeks or months, not years.

It's possible to grieve too long. Depending on your personality and coping mechanisms, you might be tempted to shrug it off like it didn't matter or hold onto the pain like a flotation device as you flounder in the sea of your tears. It's good to be emotional, but allow your emotions to be governed by wisdom and (most importantly) by the Holy Spirit.

### #3: Don't Try to Be Best Friends with Your Ex

I say "best friends" because I don't believe it is impossible to maintain a healthy friendship after a dating breakup for Christians. But I do think in most cases it should not be attempted. I think you have to consider how serious the relationship was. If you went on a date in high school with a girl and now you are in the same marriage Bible study with both your spouses, relax. It doesn't need to be a big deal.

But if you had a long-term dating relationship with someone that was serious, it's not healthy to try and remain friends. The heart just doesn't work like that. You will ruin each other's future dating chances, you'll slow the healing process, and you'll probably have to fight unnecessary temptation as a result.

Social media can be a killer when it comes to moving on. I recommend resisting the temptation to remain social media buddies. You don't have to be enemies, but if you want to move on in a healthy way, you'll need to be intentional about boundaries. The risk-reward just isn't worth it. Not to mention how uncomfortable this continued relationship could make your future spouse.

## #4: Confess Your Part, Forgive His/Her Wrongs, Repent, and Keep Moving Forward

If you get the chance during the actual breakup process, ask your ex for forgiveness in relation to any sins you committed against him or her. Small or big, own your part and repent first to God and then to the person you hurt.

Also take intentional time to forgive your ex of any sins against you. It's ideal if he or she asks for that forgiveness, but their participation is not necessary for you to forgive.

The important thing is to do it. Nothing ruins your future relationships more than an offense you haven't forgiven against someone in your past. You'll project that hurt onto the wrong source of your pain, you will mistrust people who should be trusted, and you'll never be able to be vulnerable again unless you forgive the people in your past who have hurt you. It may sound cliché, but it's true: forgiving someone is setting yourself free.

If you never take the time to analyze what you did wrong in the relationship, you will never change. If you never take the time to forgive their wrongs, you will never truly move forward. Not every relationship ended because of sin. But we all sin during relationships. God wants to use your breakup to grow and sanctify you. After you repent, embrace God's forgiveness and restoration by moving on without shame (2 Corinthians 7:10, 1 John 1:9).

## Be Intentional

In closing, don't underestimate the importance of navigating the rough waters that will follow after a breakup. If you're in a water current, you will be swept downriver but you can still navigate your boat. You'll just have to be intentional. Otherwise you will be at the mercy of the waters. The same is true during the weeks and months after a breakup.

After a breakup, God wants to graciously heal you and prepare you for the future. Believe the best of God, grieve well, set healthy boundaries, and use that past relationship as a learning experience.

# Study Questions

1. Breakups are usually never easy, but they can be done in a healthy way. What does a healthy breakup look like to you?

2. Do you think people who use to date should remain friends? Does it matter how serious the relationship was? Explain your answers.

3. How can unforgiveness towards people in your past ruin your future relationships?

# Chapter 17

# How to Forgive Someone Who Has Hurt You Deeply

How do you forgive someone who has hurt you deeply? Sadly this is a question every human will have to answer if they hope to keep their heart healthy.

If you are single now but hope to be in a romantic relationship someday, some of the best preparation you can do will be to learn how to be forgiving. During our season of singleness, one of the things that often happens is that we begin to idealize what our future relationship will be like. No one fantasizes over arguing with their future spouse. But if you really want a great future marriage one day, you will be wise to learn about forgiveness during your singleness. If you hope to love anyone, the possibility for hurt will never leave and thus forgiveness will always be deeply needed.

The first step in forgiving someone who has hurt you deeply is to prepare in advance before the hurt even happens.

### Prepare in Advance to Forgive Someone "When" They Hurt You Deeply

It's interesting how Peter phrases the question in Mathew 18:21, "Lord, how often will my brother sin against me, and I forgive him?" Jesus and Peter's conversation is not a hypothetical "if" someone sins against you. It's a factual assumption made clear with the words that our brothers and sisters "will sin" against us. C.S. Lewis states:

"To love at all is to be vulnerable. Love anything and your heart will be wrung and possibly broken. If you want to make sure of keeping it intact you must give it to no one, not even an animal. Wrap it carefully round with hobbies and little luxuries; avoid all entanglements. Lock it up safe in the casket or coffin of your selfishness. But in that casket, safe, dark, motionless, airless, it will change. It will not be broken; it will become unbreakable, impenetrable, irredeemable. To love is to be vulnerable."

And so we can begin to see why Jesus spent so much time teaching us to forgive one another. You see, divorces don't happen after years of sinning and cruelty towards one another. Divorces happen after years of sinning and cruelty towards one another without there being any repentance and forgiveness.

The main difference between a healthy friendship and a broken friendship is that one friendship is committed to forgiving the offenses and moving on in love and the other friendship never forgives and thus can never move on.

Church splits don't happen because members of the church hurt each other, rebel against the pastor, or because of sin. Church splits happen when the people of God are not willing to admit their sins, repent, and are not eager to forgive one another when these things do happen, because eventually they will.

Therefore, to forgive those who have hurt us deeply, we will be much better equipped if we have prepared our hearts before the hurt even occurs, knowing forgiveness will eventually be needed.

## Forgive Imperfect People Who Have Hurt You Deeply Because of Your Perfect God

Jesus knows from experience that if you want to be happy in your relationships it's not going to happen by finding perfect people who never let you down.

When Jesus was betrayed by Peter, Jesus didn't write him off forever and say, "You know . . . I was wrong about you. You've really hurt me deeply. I was planning on starting my church with you. But now that you sinned against me, it's over!"

No, before Peter betrayed Jesus, Jesus predicted he would deny him three times. Jesus was already planning on forgiving him before the offense ever took place (Luke 22:32). Jesus knew the only way he would be able to have a relationship with those he loved would be if he was willing to forgive them often.

And so all this raises the question that Jesus is going to answer for us. If people are going to hurt us deeply, even the people who we love the most, how can we protect ourselves from becoming, as C.S. Lewis said, hard hearted people who never risk being vulnerable? How can we avoid becoming the type of people who protect themselves from hurt by choosing to feel nothing, but in the process they also cut themselves off from feeling love? How are we going to find the motivation to love those who don't deserve it? How are we to forgive people after we have already forgiven them so many times before?

The answer is found in Matthew 18:33, "Shouldn't you have had mercy on your fellow servant just as I had on you?" The way you will find the love to forgive those who have hurt you deeply is by basing your love not in the one who wronged you but in the One who has never wronged you – God.

The only way you will be able to forgive your fellow servant after he sins against you again and again is to do it for the sake of the Master who has forgiven you again and again. To have the motivation to forgive others of much you will have to do it out of your gratitude for the One who has forgiven you much more.

Because we are eager for the full redemption that awaits us even though we don't deserve it, we should be eager to give this relational redemption to those who are in our debt.

**Because We Are Secure in God's Love, We Can Be Vulnerable in Our Love of Others**

For God's sake, not for people's sake, are we to forgive unconditionally as he forgives us unconditionally. Because Jesus was secure in the love of his Father and sought to please him above all else, he was free to forgive even when others did not deserve it. Jesus was able to be vulnerable with the people he knew were going to hurt him deeply because he was so secure in the love of God. This is what he now expects of us.

To reflect and glorify God, we must forgive those who have hurt us deeply. And to forgive those who have hurt us deeply, our motivation must be to reflect and glorify God.

# Study Questions

1. Why is it so important to learn how to forgive during your season of singleness if you hope to have a healthy marriage one day?

2. What does our willingness or unwillingness to forgive people say about our relationship with God?

3. How can you be vulnerable while still protecting your own heart? How does forgiveness help us stay vulnerable and thus able to love?

# Chapter 18

## How to Avoid the #1 Danger for Most Unmarried Christians

What is the greatest danger for most unmarried Christians? And how do single Christians avoid this danger?

To answer these questions, it helps to know that all of God's commands are meant for his glory and our good. God knows the best thing for us is to first love him above all things. Secondly, he calls us to love people as well (Matthew 22:38-39). Therefore, it is safe to conclude that loving God is the best thing for us and loving people is the second best thing for us.

If you were to reverse the order of these commands, however, you would quickly find yourself in sinful idolatry of people over God. When we don't do the first command, abusing the second command is actually the easiest thing to do.

Again, God said his commands are good for us (Deuteronomy 10:13). Therefore, it makes perfect sense that when our love of God is absent, we literally feel empty inside and lonely because we are missing out on all the good God wants for us that comes through our love for him. No one can live long while doing nothing to fill this emptiness they feel. Since loving people is the second greatest commandment, which means it must be the second best thing for us, is it any wonder that if God is not really our God, people quickly become the greatest temptation and danger to our hearts?

Of all of God's creation, people reflect God's image most. It should be no surprise, then, that when our hearts ache for God but go without finding him, they quickly attach themselves to people because they are literally the next best thing to God himself.

The strongest lure away from God is the love of man, especially romantic love. There are only two restrictions on romantic relationships in the Bible. One, if you are married, to only be in romantic relationship with your spouse. Two, if you are single, to only pursue a romantic relationships with another Christian who would make a good, godly spouse (1 Corinthians 7:39, 2 Corinthians 6:14).

This is why for unmarried people, the most dangerous and tempting sin will be to attach themselves to an unbelieving person. In the context of loving God and seeking a Christian spouse to love and be loved by, there is zero problems. God wants the vast majority of his people to get married. He wants those marriages to be Christ-centered so spouses can help one another love God. Non-Christians have no desire to love Christ.

So to summarize, it's right to love God, it's right to love people, and it's right to pursue a spouse who will help you love God first and people second. But if you don't love God and are not pursuing a Christian spouse, the greatest temptation will be to link up with a non-believer since they still reflect God's image to some degree and are thus the most alluring solution to fulfilling the needs within.

In Nehemiah 13, Nehemiah goes to the extreme, even coming across as abusive to our 21st century consciousness. However, he rebuked the people so harshly because he knew their sin of marrying godless spouses was really that dangerous. Just as God's commands are given to us in love, so are our Lord's corrections and consequences (Hebrews 12:7-11). Nehemiah's extreme reaction to romantic relationships with godless people shows how extremely dangerous these relationships are to Christ's people.

To be clear, idolizing people will be a struggle for everyone. When you are married, you can easily idolize your spouse or kids or someone else just as easily as you idolized people when you were single. But to answer the question posed, "How do you avoid the biggest danger to an unmarried Christian?" the short answer is this: Pursue God and pursue a Christian spouse, as both of these pursuits are God honoring.

If you are not loving God and not pursuing a godly spouse who loves Christ, which are both good and biblical things to do, you will have an unstoppable desire to fill the need within you. The thing that comes closest to these genuine needs of the heart is an unbelieving person, therefore a romantic relationship with an unbeliever is the most dangerous temptation for an unmarried Christian.

(Note: As discussed earlier in this book, there is a biblical category for lifelong singleness. One indicator that will be present for those who are called to singleness is that they will not even have the desire for marriage (1 Corinthians 7:9, 37). This lack of desire will not be rooted in fear or the result of abuse, but rather the person will simply desire to live a celibate life solely to pursue God. However, this chapter was written assuming the single person has a desire for marriage, which is an indicator God has designed them to be married.)

# Study Questions

1. Do you agree that the greatest danger for most unmarried Christians is a romantic relationship with an unbeliever? Why or why not?

2. Why does God give us commands? Why does God command Christians not to marry unbelievers (1 Corinthians 7:39, 2 Corinthians 6:14)?

3. What changes in a person when they become a Christian? What different desires do believers and unbelievers have?

# Chapter 19

# What Does the Bible Say About Missionary Dating?

Should Christians date unbelievers? After all, if you are a Christian, can't you seek to bring someone to Jesus through dating? God has used "missionary dating" for some, so why not for you?

As a single Christian, one of the questions which can dominate the thoughts is, "Who will I marry?" With so little Christians in the world, and even fewer who share the same interests as you, the odds are certainly stacked against a Christian guy or Christian girl seeking a good relational fit.

The temptation is understandable, therefore, to look outside of the church at unbelievers, looking for anyone with common interests who is relatable to you, regardless if they are a Christian or not.

## Missionary Dating Crosses God's Line

As tempting as it is to missionary date, the best dating advice is simple: Do it God's way!

The Bible is very clear on this matter. Christians are to be a light to the world, they are to spread the gospel of Jesus Christ, and they are supposed to love unbelievers in word and deed. But they are also never to be "unequally yoked with unbelievers" (2 Corinthians 6:14).

Jesus spent time with unsaved sinners, loved them, and even served them; but he never called them his friends. He was "friendly" towards them, but that is different than opening your heart to someone and forming a "friendship with the world." While God calls us to love the world, he also commands us to guard our own hearts (Proverbs 4:23), to be aware of the damage people can cause us who are not lovers of God (James 4:4), and to "not be misled: 'Bad company corrupts good character'" (1 Corinthians 15:33). As much as we might be attracted to someone not saved, we must remember how impossible it is for an unbeliever to please God:

> "For to set the mind on the flesh is death, but to set the mind on the Spirit is life and peace. For the mind that is set on the flesh is hostile to God, for it does not submit to God's law; indeed, it cannot. Those who are in the flesh cannot please God." (Romans 8:6-8)

If we hope to please God, we must not be yoked with those still in the flesh (unbelievers) because it is impossible for someone without the Holy Spirit to please God. And dating someone definitely yokes you.

## Missionary Dating Always Results in Negative Consequences

While facts like these may be plain, what can be confusing is that missionary dating seems to have worked for other Christians that we may know. There are real cases of people who started dating an unbeliever, but then that person got saved, and now the two of them are enjoying a wonderful Christian marriage.

While that may be true, this fact is true as well: Whenever we disobey God's word, there is always a natural consequence. While God forgives us of our sins and turns our evil mistakes into good through the gospel of Jesus Christ, there are still natural consequences that remain. (For example: With gluttony, the fat calories are going to negatively affect your body even though God forgives you for this sin when you repent.) Therefore, if someone does missionary date and it "works out," while God was pleased to use his grace to create a good end result, there will be negative consequences to bear for the sinful means that were taken.

For example, it's highly unlikely that a brand new Christian will have the maturity to resist the sexual temptation that will be presented through the dating season. Sexual sin during the dating phase will certainly affect the marriage season. Without a season for the new believer to grow in their personal relationship with God before entering into a romantic relationship, there will be many growing pains the more mature Christian will have to endure because of the lack of Christian maturity their partner possesses. God's grace will redeem all our sins, but there will also be self-inflicted trials on us when we deviate from God's ways.

Additionally, while it is impossible to know if someone will turn from the faith and prove themselves to never truly have been saved, there is a higher probability for a new convert to turn compared with someone who has a track record of faithfulness with God.

Perseverance and endurance are the marks of true believers, and these evidences can only be revealed through time. While there is no guarantee that anyone we marry will not turn out to be a false convert later in life, there is a greater likely hood of more mature Christians remaining faithful to God while new converts are more likely to fall away, proving they were never truly saved to begin with. Therefore, to marry a new believer is putting yourself at a greater risk of marrying someone who will later turn and reveal themselves as no Christian at all.

## Missionary Dating Is Not Needed Because God Is More Than Able

Missionary dating is not needed because God is able to give you a spouse and save people without deviating from his word. While God may save someone through missionary dating, he is also able to save through many other healthy means.

Additionally, it always presents a poor witness when a Christian is willing to go directly against God's written word for the sake of someone else. A better witness than missionary dating is to share the love of Christ with unbelievers while not disobeying God's word. It sends a very odd message when you try to tell someone they should obey what God has said in the Bible, but your relationship with that person is in direct disobedience to what the Bible says.

If a relationship like this does "work out," when the new Christian and the older Christian are presented with tough biblical choices, the newer Christian may expect the older Christian to bend on obeying the word of God just as he or she did at the beginning of their relationship. If the newer Christian is not ready to tithe, to raise their children in the Lord, to attend church regularly as a family, or do one of the other many difficult things the Bible commands Christians to do, the newer Christian will look at their partner (the missionary dater) and expect him or her to follow along in a lukewarm walk which the relationship was founded on.

While missionary dating seems to have worked for some, there will always be consequences in that marriage for its unbiblical beginning. Perhaps God does want to save an unbeliever who will then become your spouse. But to rush ahead of God, not giving him the time to do what he wants in the way he wants is to rob yourself of the blessings he desires to give and to set yourself up for difficulties in marriage that could have been avoided.

*"A woman is bound to her husband as long as he lives. But if her husband dies, she is free to marry anyone she wishes, but he must belong to the Lord.-Corinthians 7:39*

*"Did not Solomon king of Israel sin on account of such women? Among the many nations there was no king like him, and he was beloved by his God, and God made him king over all Israel. Nevertheless, foreign women made even him to sin."*
*-Nehemiah 13:26*

## Study Questions

1. Even though missionary dating has "worked out" for some, there are always consequences when we disobey God's word. If God wants to make an unbeliever into a believer and then have you marry him or her, he can do this without you dating that person while he or she is an unbeliever. Do you agree or disagree with this logic? Why or why not?

2. What do you think it says to unbelievers when a believer is willing to disobey God to date him or her?

3. How can you be a witness to unbelievers of the opposite sex without letting your heart become romantically attached to them?

# Chapter 20

# Let God Fulfill God's Promises to You

Imagine a man who loved a woman, but he was going off to war and he didn't know when he would be back. Before he left he promised her that when he returned, he would marry her. How odd would it be if the woman jumped the gun and went out and bought her own engagement ring? She wanted the promise to be fulfilled, but she did not want to wait, so she took matters into her own hands.

God is a God of promises. He promises good for those who love him. He promises to save those who put their faith in Jesus. He promises to take care of us when we trust him.  Throughout nearly every page of Scripture, a promise can be found that was made by God.

During our season of singleness, so many blessings seem distant and far off in the future. The temptation is to try and take control of our lives in sinful ways that usurp God's authority and timing.

Life is a journey. The path to God is straight and narrow (Matthew 7:14). But throughout the journey of life there are so many ways to veer away from God. Perhaps one of the most common ways is to seek God's promises and blessings in your own power.

### You Can't Fulfill God's Promises in Your Own Power

Humans are naturally impatient. God gives us promises or puts a good desire in our heart, and because he does not fulfill it as quickly as we want, so often we take matters into our own hands. This always leads to sin.

As you read through Genesis 15-18, the order of the events is shocking. In Genesis 15:4-6, God promises Abraham an offspring who will be multiplied into a vast nation. Abraham believed God, but when we come to Genesis 16:1-2, apparently Abraham and his wife felt that they needed to help God fulfill his promise through their own power. So, they took Hagar, Sarah's slave, and gave her to Abraham. Hagar became pregnant with a son, Ishmael.

This was not how God wanted to fulfill his promise. For in Genesis 17:18-19 it states, "And Abraham said to God, 'Oh that Ishmael might live before you!' God said, 'No, but Sarah your wife shall bear you a son, and you shall call his name Isaac. I will establish my covenant with him as an everlasting covenant for his offspring after him."

They had a great promise from God, but they veered from God's path by trying to fulfill that promise themselves in their own power. In Genesis 18:13-14, it states:

> "The LORD said to Abraham, "Why did Sarah laugh and say, 'Shall I indeed bear a child, now that I am old?' Is anything too hard for the LORD? At the appointed time I will return to you, about this time next year, and Sarah shall have a son."

Let's quickly recap the events. It all starts when God promises Abraham a son but does not tell him when this will happen, Sarah and Abraham take matters into their own hands and produce a son through Hagar, and then God reveals that this was not what he wanted because he had an "appointed time." When God finally told Abraham a specific time that Isaac was to be born (Genesis 18:14), Ishmael was at least thirteen years old (Genesis 17:25). Abraham and Sarah should have waited at least thirteen years longer and then God would have fulfilled the promise himself.

If you read the whole story for yourself, you'll see that because Abraham tried to fulfill God's promise in his own power, huge problems occurred that could have been avoided. The same is always true in our lives as well.

If you are single, God probably has a spouse for you. God isn't, however, going to show you when he is going to bring that person into your life. So many get off track by taking matters into their own hands by dating non-Christians, by settling for the wrong type of person, or by going into a black hole of depression rather than getting out there so God can bless them.

When we take matters into our own hands like this, we always create extra conflict for ourselves that we could have avoided. God can be trusted. He's powerful enough to fulfill his own promises. We just need to give him the time to do what he has already committed to do but only at his "appointed time."

## You Will Be Greatly Blessed When You Wait for God to Fulfill His Own Promise

In 1 Samuel 16 God promised David that he would be king. He was just a boy then, and there were going to be many twists and turns before that promise was going to be fulfilled.

As David grew into a man, surely he could sense that the promise was getting close to fulfillment. He had killed Goliath, won many great military campaigns, people were starting to gather to him and leave Saul, and everyone could see the writing on the wall that Saul was losing his kingdom and David was eventually going to be the king.

David's commitment to the Lord was tested when David could have killed Saul. Saul wandered into a cave where Dave and his men were, and David's men urged him to kill Saul and take the kingdom for himself. David could have assumed this was his time to fulfill God's promise. Hadn't he waited long enough? Hadn't he done enough for God? How much longer would he have to wait to take hold of that which God had promised him so many years ago?

Rather than take matters into his own hands, David let Saul live. After Saul left the cave, David called to him, "May the LORD judge between me and you, may the LORD avenge me against you, but my hand shall not be against you. . . . May the LORD therefore be judge and give sentence between me and you, and see to it and plead my cause and deliver me from your hand" (1 Samuel 24:12, 15).

In the end, David made the right decision. Not only did he eventually become king as God had promised, he avoided turning from God through the process, thus also avoiding all kinds of trouble for himself.

We must, through the grace of God, seek to do the same in our lives. God has promised many amazing things to us both in his word and to us personally. Rarely, however, does God's timetable match our expectations. The only thing we accomplish by taking matters into our own hands is creating huge, unnecessary problems for ourselves.

God is powerful enough to fulfill his own promises. Surely he will lead us to do certain things in life so we can receive those promises. None of what I am saying is meant to encourage us to just sit on the couch and watch the clock. But we need to seek God and remain close to him so we have the wisdom and direction to not take matters into our own hands.

God can fulfill his own promises for you. Trust him. He is worthy.

> *"The Lord visited Sarah as he had said, and the Lord did to Sarah as he had promised."*
> *-Genesis 21:1*

## Study Questions

1. If you want to be married, how are you doing during this waiting period? Are you tempted to take matters into your own hands and stop trusting God?

2. What is the difference between "taking matters into your own hands" and being an active participant in taking hold of God's blessings? How does obeying God's commands help us stay on track?

3. Pursuing good things in bad ways leads to sin, but sometimes it's hard to tell when we are doing this ourselves? How can other people in our lives help us avoid this problem?

# Chapter 21

# Does God Need Our Help? No, But He Does Ask for It

Two plain truths can be seen from a simple reading of the Bible: God can do whatever he wants. And God asks us to do things.

These two truths make me ask, "Why does God ask for help if he doesn't need it?" At first glance it seems one of these two truths must be false for the other to be true. If God can do whatever he wants in his own power, then clearly he must not ask us to do things for him. Or, if God does ask us to do things for him, clearly he must not be able to do things on his own.

So which is it? Does God need our help?

**God Does Not Need Our Help**

Call it what you will: sovereignty, power, omnipotent, ordained, self-sufficient, eternal, without need, being God. Whatever words we want to use to describe it, the clear reality found in Scripture is that God doesn't need anything, including our help.

> "The God who made the world and everything in it, being Lord of heaven and earth, does not live in temples made by man, nor is he served by human hands, as though he needed anything, since he himself gives to all mankind life and breath and everything." (Acts 17:24-25)

"If I were hungry, I would not tell you, for the world and its fullness are mine." (Psalm 50:12)

"Our God is in the heavens; he does all that he pleases." (Psalm 115:3)

"Whatever the LORD pleases, he does, in heaven and on earth, in the seas and all deeps." (Psalm 135:6)

**Although God Has No Needs, He Does Ask for Our Help**

While these Scriptures undeniably point out that God does not need us, we could list hundreds of Scriptures where God tells us to do things for him. For example, Jesus said:

"All authority in heaven and on earth has been given to me. Go therefore and make disciples of all nations, baptizing them in the name of the Father and of the Son and of the Holy Spirit, teaching them to observe all that I have commanded you. And behold, I am with you always, to the end of the age." (Matthew 28:18-20)

Here we can see that Jesus has all the authority to do whatever he wants. But he also tells us to assist him in building his kingdom. So it's safe to say that God does ask for our help.

God doesn't ask for our help in the sense that he needs us to do something that he can't do without us. He "asks for our help" in the sense that he has invited us to participate in his divine agenda and even allows important tasks to go unfinished if we do not do the jobs he has asked us to do.

When it comes to your development during your season of singleness or the process of meeting your future spouse, God invites you to participate. He's not going to wave a magic wand. He is in control and he has a plan, but that doesn't mean you don't have an active part to play.

### If God Doesn't Need Us, Why Did He Create Us and Command Us to Serve Him?

So these two truths can coexist. God does not need us, but God does use us. All this begs the question, "Why?"

We could offer endless answers here, but I think the overarching answer can be summed up this way: God asks us to serve him because he loves us.

If God doesn't need our help, and yet he asks for our help, perhaps he does this not for his needs but because of ours. God doesn't need us, we need God. And this is true even when it comes to our service of him. God doesn't need us to accomplish tasks for him (Psalm 115:3). A needed characteristic of divinity is sovereignty. You can't claim to be God if you don't have the power to do whatever you want on your own. Therefore, it's safe to conclude that God relies on humans to accomplish certain tasks not for his need but for ours.

We need to need God. Okay, that's a confusing way to put it. In other words, we wouldn't be living the best existence possible if we were not living for God. God knows he is the best, and therefore to create us for any lesser purpose other than to serve him would have been cruel. God is not showing his neediness when he created humans and then commanded us to serve him. God created us out of his fullness, not his emptiness.

God was eternally fulfilled within his Triune relationship. He created us not because something was missing from his joy, but because his joy and love was so full it would have been selfish not to freely share it. God created us to serve him because it was the most loving thing to do. God is the best, serving God is the best, and therefore God made us for this purpose.

## God Allows Us to Help Him for Our Good

Lastly, God includes us in his agenda for our good. I can clean up my three year old son's bedroom ten times faster than him. It's actually much easier for me to do it myself rather than to get him to do it. He takes forever. I have to keep encouraging him to do it, reminding him of the rewards he will get if he listens to me, reminding him of the discipline he will receive if he doesn't listen to me, I have to point out where the toys should go, and I have to help him lift things that are too heavy.

So why don't I just clean his room for him if I don't need him to help me? I make him help me because it's good for him, not because I need his help. I can pick up his toys in one minute if I wanted to. I really don't need the help of a three year old to do anything. But what kind of father would I be if I never included him? While it might be easier for me to not ask for his help, it's better for his development that I do.

Additionally, he oftentimes enjoys helping me. Just the other day when I was staining the fence, he wanted to help. Again, his "help" actually slowed me down. But it was a way for us to grow as father and son and it was good for him.

Likewise, this is one of the reasons why God uses humans at all. God doesn't need our help, but he knows it's good for us to work with him. It will bring God and us joy. He can accomplish his agenda in a moment. And yet he waits patiently for us to do what he's asked, reminding us of the rewards we will get if we listen to him, reminding us of the discipline we will receive if we don't listen to him, he has to point out where we should go to serve him, and he has to help us lift things that are too heavy.

Paul wrote the Philippians and made it known that it was good of them to help him, but he clarified his motivation when he said, "Not that I seek the gift, but I seek the fruit that increases to your credit" (Philippians 4:17). Paul imitated God by asking others to help him not for his own good but for theirs.

God doesn't ultimately ask you for help because he wants more from you, but he invites you to give gifts to him for your good, so your fruit will "increase to your credit." God certainly doesn't need our help, but he does ask for it because he loves us.

So as you move forward in your season of singleness or as you begin the dating process, remember that God is in control while also inviting you to participate for your own good.

## Study Questions

1. If someone asked you, "If God is totally in control of everything, why does he tell us to do things?" how would you answer?

2. Is it comforting or confusing to you when you think about God's sovereignty? How do you feel when you think about the fact that God has a plan for your relationships?

3. What might you never learn if God did everything for you without requiring you to be active?

# Chapter 22

# How to Find a Christian Mentor in Your Season of Singleness

In every Christian, whether they would admit it or not, there is a desire to have a strong, wise mentor who is willing to invest in them. Few, however, find a wiser Christian mentor who is willing to help guide them through life, relationships, and ministry as a good mentor should.

There are few things as helpful during your season of singleness than a good mentor who has been in your shoes before. He can explain what he did in similar circumstances. She can loving correct you when she sees you making mistakes. And he or she can be there for you when you just don't know what to do.

So how do you find a Christian mentor?

## How to Find a Christian Mentor: Don't Be Self-Centered

"Where are all the mentors?" is often posed as a question but it is really meant to be an accusation against the generation above us. But perhaps the blame does not always lie in the lack of mentors available but also in the demands and expectations of those desiring to be mentored.

In our early years, especially amongst the millennial generation (which I am one), out of the love many of our parents have for us, they did all they could to give us the best chance of maturing into responsible adults.

They footed the bill and sacrificed every weekend for 10 years straight so we could be on that travel sports team. Our coach came prepared to practices and games with a plan to help us succeed.

Some of our parents worked an extra job to get us to the best high school possible. We live in a society where the teachers are expected to help and pour into the students.

Students then go off to college and there again the expectation is for the professors to go above and beyond to help the student who needs the help. In all of these different contexts, often times these parents, coaches, and teachers are even blamed for the younger person's lack of success.

In none of these scenarios is the child, player, or student expected to be an asset to the parent, coach, teacher, or professor. In the Bible, however, those being mentored or apprenticed were actually useful to the mentor.

Paul had many younger men in his life that he was mentoring, but all of these men were also working towards the same goal as Paul during the mentoring process. Paul had a singular focus in advancing the gospel of Jesus Christ and when anyone started to hinder this goal, even young men in need of mentoring, Paul cut ties with them for the sake of the larger mission.

In Acts 15:37-39 we learn that Mark is becoming a distraction to Paul because Mark is struggling to stay committed to the missionary work Paul was doing. Therefore, even though Mark clearly could have benefited from some extra mentoring by Paul to help him with his commitment problems, Paul thought it was best to not take Mark along anymore.

## Join the Ministry of the Mentor, Don't Expect to Be the Ministry

Perhaps the reason there are so few mentoring relationships happening now days is because those who are in need of being mentored expect older people to drop their entire life and revolve themselves around the mentored. Often times the mentored want to be the ministry rather than join a mentor in a ministry.

This is the opposite approach Paul used with his mentoring relationships. He did not join their direction in life but rather invited them to join him in his direction.

Likewise, Jesus did not start following the disciples, asking Peter and John when would be convenient for them for him to stop by and give them the eight magical steps to be better fishermen. Rather, Jesus told them to follow him so he could teach them to advance his kingdom. The disciples joined Jesus' mission and direction in life, Jesus didn't join their mission and direction in life.

## Be an Asset to Your Mentor, Not a VDP

Typically, the types of older Christian men and women we would want to be mentored by are active, busy Christians who are showing they have great direction and purpose in life. Christian CEOs, great coaches, pastors, or admirable parents, if they are any good at what they are doing, should be busy running their companies, studying their sports, shepherding their flocks, and attending to their families, all for the glory of God. Christian mentors like these don't have time for people who are going to distract them from their primary goals.

But, usually, Christian mentors do have time to train people to accomplish similar goals which they hold. Goal driven people are typically willing to allow others to walk beside them if that person will actually help them in their life's passion and work.

A great Christian mom is much more likely to take a young wife under her tutelage if the younger woman will come over during the day and help the older woman clean the house, allowing them time to talk as they fold the mounds of laundry the older women needs to get done before the kids come home from school.

A great pastor will be much more willing to mentor a young man if that young man is willing to meet and help him manage the church youth ministry once a week.

The Christian CEO might let a MBA intern join her inner circle if that student is willing to be available whenever the phone rings, makes copies without complaining, gets coffee the way she likes it, and does whatever else she and the other board members ask.

Successful, busy people simply avoid VDPs (very draining people). You may think a Christian should just be willing to help anyone who needs help. But God gifts each Christian differently. Thankfully there are those who have the gift of compassion and can mentor anyone, no matter how much time and emotional energy it might take. But if you want a highly successful and accomplished Christian to be your mentor, you just can't be a VDP.

Goal driven people have internal radar that steers them as far away as possible from individuals who will be dramatic, distracting, and difficult to work with. Anything or anyone that will hinder their goals simply gets avoided like the plague.

**Put in the Work and Serve, Don't Just Expect to Be Served**

Paul wrote Timothy and Titus personal letters not just because Paul was so generous with his time (which he clearly was), but also because Timothy and Titus were useful in church planting, which was a major goal of his.

Paul was personally invested in the church at Philippi because he loved them but also "because of [their] partnership in the gospel from the first day until now" (Philippians 1:5). Paul's main goal was to glorify God by the advancement of the gospel. It is not surprising, therefore, that Paul gave extra time and attention to people and churches who shared his same passion in life.

As our life continues to unfold, a good Christian mentor is priceless in helping us journey well. So if you want to be mentored, then perhaps you need to be willing to roll up your sleeves and work, making yourself useful to the ministry your Christian mentor is already committed to rather than asking a very focused person to make you their new ministry.

*(Note: To be fair and balanced, Barnabas disagreed with Paul and wanted to still be around Mark, and the Bible does not say who was right or wrong in this disagreement. Later in 2 Timothy 4:11, once Mark matures a bit, we see Paul actually requesting Mark because now "he is very useful to me for ministry," which again proves Paul wanted to partner with people who would help his mission.*

*Perhaps Mark became a more useful person because Barnabas did go the extra mile to help a younger person who wasn't useful yet. Colossians 4:10 explains that Mark and Barnabas were cousins, so it seems logical that we should go the extra mile for people who we have a stronger commitment to such as family and close friends. Surely there is a need to help those who may not be a direct asset right away like Barnabas did for Mark. But the principle still applies that if you want to know how to find a Christian mentor, it helps to be helpful to that mentor.)*

## Study Questions

1. Have you ever been mentored before? Why was it a good or bad experience?

2. What are the benefits of having a more mature person mentor you?

3. How can you find a great mentor who has accomplished things in life that you want to accomplish?

# Section 4:

# How to Find a Christian Spouse

# Chapter 23

# How to Find a Christian Spouse

There's been a lot of advice given to Christian singles who desire to find a spouse: "Just pray about it." "Just serve Jesus and he'll take care of it." "Stop desiring to be married and then God will bless you with a Christian spouse." "Just get on a Christian dating site already and stop talking to me about this all the time!"

When it comes down to it, there seems to be two camps in the "How to find a Christian spouse" advice market. One group says just serve Jesus and it will take care of itself. The other group says God only helps those who help themselves.

So which is it? What's the best way to find a Christian spouse?

**To Find a Christian Spouse, Seek God and Be Active**

A Christian should view the process of finding a spouse no differently than how all Christians should pursue fulfilling any good desire.

The Bible instructs us to seek God and be proactive in seeking what we desire and need. Matthew 6:31-33 explains:

> "Therefore do not be anxious, saying, 'What shall we eat?' or 'What shall we drink?' or 'What shall we wear?' For the Gentiles seek after all these things, and your heavenly Father knows that you need them all. But seek first the kingdom of God and his righteousness, and all these things will be added to you."

Often times when Christian singles desire to please God, they feel they must stop pursuing a Christian spouse and solely serve God. And Bible passages like Matthew 6:31-33 seem to support this idea. At first glance, it seems that the way we get things we want from God is to stop seeking them and just seek him.

But that's not what the Bible says. Matthew 6:33 states "seek first the kingdom of God." It doesn't say to stop seeking the things you want and need. In context, Jesus is talking about material things like food and clothing. He tells us not to worry about these things. What Jesus is saying is that we should not let our desire for things overtake our desire for God. When God is first in our lives, God will bless our lives. But none of these statements mean we should be passive in our pursuit of what we want and desire. Paul says in 2 Thessalonians 3:6, 10:

> "Now we command you, brothers, in the name of our Lord Jesus Christ, that you keep away from any brother who is walking in idleness and not in accord with the tradition that you received from us. . . . If anyone is not willing to work, let him not eat."

We can apply these same principles in answering "How do I find a Christian spouse?" It's basically the same thing as asking, "How do I find the food, clothing, and things that I need." Scripture teaches us that we must put God first. We must not be anxious about our needs. But we must not be passive either.

To find a Christian spouse, you first need to put God first in your life. If you are anxious and stressed about your marital future, a time of reflection and separation from dating will do your heart good.

But to kneel at your bedside every night and wake up the next day to do nothing active in your pursuit to find a Christian spouse is not the normal pattern in Scripture when it comes to receiving blessings from God.

## Follow God, Not Your Natural Instincts

From my experience in coaching singles on how to find a Christian spouse, I've found people often do what comes most natural to them, but they do it under the guise of following God's leading.

As we discussed, it's crucial to seek God first in your search for a Christian spouse. But it's also really important to be proactive as well. Christians often attach themselves to one of these roads, and usually their choice is a reflection of their personality.

Introverts and people who are a bit shyer tend to fall into the "If I just follow Jesus, I will find a Christian spouse" camp. Extroverts and people who have a great need to be liked by the other gender usually fall into the "God blesses those who help themselves, so I've got to date as many people as possible" camp.

God may lead you to take a season off from actively pursuing a Christian spouse. But if God is calling you to marriage, this season will need to end at some point soon. Most people don't just find their spouse by dumb luck. Yes God is sovereign and ordains each of our days before we live them (Psalm 139:16), but this theological truth should never stall our practical living. God requires us to play our part, not to sit in prayer all our days. Prayer is essential, but prayer empowers us for living. Prayer should never replace living.

On the flipside, nothing (for most) is more seductive to an unmarried Christian than the opposite sex. Therefore it will be very easy to replace God with your desire for a Christian spouse. If you always have a boyfriend or girlfriend and yet you are still unmarried, a season of getting your heart right will do you good.

What's essential is that we are walking with God in our search for a Christian spouse. Don't just do what's natural. Be honest with yourself. If you're a bit shy and get nervous about dating, take the plunge and go to a single's ministry or signup for a safe Christian online dating service. And if you're always dating, take a step back so you can put God first.

Follow God, not your natural instincts.

## To Find a Christian Spouse, Pursue Your Other Desires with People

This last piece of advice is the most practical and applicational. It just make sense that if you desire to find a Christian spouse, you need to put yourself around the type of people you would like to be with in marriage.

But this never works when you just put yourself around people because you are looking for a Christian spouse. It's usually too unnatural. In C.S. Lewis' book *The Four Loves*, he talks about the importance of having things in common with people:

> "We picture lovers face to face but friends side by side; their eyes look ahead. That is why those pathetic people who simply "want friends" can never make any. The very condition of having friends is that we should want something else besides friends. . . . There would be nothing for the friendship to be about; and friendship

must be about something, even if it were only an enthusiasm for dominoes or white mice. Those who have nothing can share nothing; those who are going nowhere can have no fellow-travelers.

When the two people who thus discover that they are on the same secret road are of different sexes, the friendship which arises between them will very easily pass into erotic love. Indeed, unless they are physically repulsive to each other or unless the one or both already loves elsewhere, it is almost certain to do so sooner or later."

So if you want to find a Christian spouse, pursue your other desires too. If your main desire is to find a Christian spouse, odds are you will not be a very interesting person. Don't be defined by your singleness. Become the person God has designed you to be, and then you will be the most attractive and desirable person possible.

So how can you find a Christian spouse? Pursue God first, be active in your search, and pursue your other desires too.

# Study Questions

1. What camp do you naturally gravitate towards? Do you feel safer just praying and not being active? Or can you only relax if you are putting maximum effort into finding a spouse? How can you be intentional about following God and not your natural instincts?

2. Do you think it is important to pursue multiple desires other than just finding a spouse while you are single? How does pursuing other interests actually help your dating chances?

3. Write a prayer to God asking him to guide you. Ask him to help you to not follow your natural instincts but rather to follow him first and foremost. If you are comfortable, ask a friend (or group member) to pray with you that God will make clear what path he would have you take in your life right now when it comes to pursuing or not pursuing a spouse.

# Chapter 24

# 6 Possible Reasons You're Still Not Married

Finding someone to marry seems like a mysterious process. And in some ways it really is. The path to meeting your future spouse will be full of twists and turns. If you are called to marriage, however, God knows just how he is going to bring your future husband or wife into your life.

While Christian singles certainly must trust and submit to the sovereignty of God, that doesn't mean God has not outlined specific actions that will increase your chances of getting married. While finding "the one" will always have elements of mystery to it, there are also many more practical elements we can look at that influence finding someone you are compatible with. There are always reasons for everything, including why you are not married.

What follows is not an exhaustive list of possible reasons you're not married. These are just some of the most common reasons for why many Christians are still single.

### Reason 1: It's Just Not Your Time to Be Married Yet

If you are a Christian, you want to be married, and you know marriage is a good gift from God, it's hard to not feel like you are doing something wrong if you are still not married. But that's not always the case.

Just because you are not married doesn't mean you are failing. It could just mean it's not your time yet. It's impossible to know all the reasons why God makes some wait until their forty to find a spouse and he allows others to get married at nineteen. The best answer is that it's just not the right time for some.

What's often forgotten is that singleness is not a biblical curse. Singleness is actually a high calling in the Bible. God instructs us that singles are often better equipped to serve him (1 Corinthians 7:32-35). Therefore, one reason you might not be married yet is because God's plan of service for you in this season can be better accomplished in singleness. Perhaps when God's call on you will be better accomplished as a married person, he will bless you with a spouse.

We don't always know the reason why some are still unmarried, but we do know that whether a Christian is single or married, God always has a good work for him or her to do (Ephesians 2:10). Singleness is a gift to be used in service to God. It might not be your time to get married, but it's always your time to serve God.

## Reason 2: You're Called to Singleness, Not Marriage

Everyone has the responsibility to use their season of singleness to serve God. However, some have the high calling of using singleness their entire life to serve God. Therefore one of the main reasons many (not most) Christian singles are not married is because they're called to a life of singleness.

I think the American Church in general has done a poor job of celebrating Christian singleness. In fact, the subtle feeling you often get from some church cultures is that it's shameful to be single, as though you are definitely doing something wrong if you are over thirty-years-old and still single.

The Bible sends the opposite message. Paul actually gives the impression that singleness is a higher calling than marriage because it's a way of life that provides more practical benefits of focusing solely on serving Jesus Christ (1 Corinthians 7:38). However, if you read 1 Corinthians 7 in its full context, Paul's message is not that singleness is better than marriage. Rather serving Jesus first and foremost is always better. Therefore whether single or married, all Christians should pursue the practical benefits of a simplified life when seeking to serve God.

You can be a single person and waist your life on worldly concerns or be a married person and use your life for kingdom purposes. The point is not that singleness or marriage is better. The point is that serving Jesus is best.

We all must embrace the life that helps us to best accomplish God's goals for us, whether that means a life of singleness or of Christian marriage.

### Reason 3: Your Sin Is Blocking God's Blessing

While it's sometimes true that the reason you're not married is simply that it's not your time, this is not the case for everyone. Marriage is a blessing from God (along with singleness), and nothing blocks God's blessings like unrepentant sin (Galatians 6:7-9).

God often withholds blessings when we are living in sin because he loves us so much. To bless us while we are in rebellion is to passively support our sinfulness. God will do what's best for us, and he knows it's always best that we repent of sin and turn to him. Therefore, to accomplish our everlasting joy in him, he will often supernaturally work against our superficial happiness rooted in idolatry and worldliness.

Therefore one reason you're not married could be that God loves you too much to bless you with a godly spouse when you are living a godless life. He absolutely wants us to have maximum joy, but he knows sin is the chief thief of true joy, which is always the joy rooted in God.

## Reason 4: Your Sinful Life Doesn't Match Your Marriage Standards, Causing Dating Paralysis

Living in sin not only affects the spiritual side in our search for a spouse. It also has very negative practical effects on a Christian who desires marriage.

If a Christian is living in sin, they will feel guilty. A Christian can be backsliding and even live in sin for a period of time. But if someone feels no guilt for their sin and thus they never fight against the sin they are stuck in, this is biblical evidence that they are not a Christian.

Therefore, if you are a Christian living in sin, you will feel guilty. This guilt wreaks havoc on your dating choices. One reason many Christians are not married is because they feel too guilty to date a Christian guy or girl who is not living in sin. So they end up dating impassionate Christians, missionary dating non-Christians, or not dating at all.

Living in sin is a major reason why many are not married because it causes Christian singles to live in a state of paralysis. You feel guilty and unworthy, so you date people who don't passionately love Jesus because you think someone who did love Jesus could never love someone like you. But since you are a Christian, you know it's wrong to marry someone who places Jesus so low on their priority list. Thus you get stuck in a cycle of feeling too unworthy to date a good Christian, but

since you love Jesus, your standards are too high to marry
someone who doesn't passionately love Jesus.

This same cycle can occur for someone who has not embraced
the full redemption offered in the gospel, which causes them to
hold onto the shame stemming from their past. Since they feel
unworthy, they don't want to open themselves to Christian men
or women who seem so much purer than them. The reason
people don't date is often because of past shame and a poor
understanding of godly purity.

The only solution to all this is to stop living in sin and embrace
the life-changing power of the gospel.

**Reason 5: You're Dating Too Much Or You're Not Dating
Enough to Find a Spouse**

As discussed earlier, Christian dating advice usually falls into
one of two categories. You are instructed to either, "Just serve
Jesus and he'll bring you a spouse" or you are told that "God
only helps those who help themselves, so get out there and
date, date, date until you find the one."

There are biblical grounds for a healthy version of both camps.
Loving Jesus Christ is always the first step to embracing his
call on your life. But that doesn't mean God doesn't call us to
action in the process of receiving his blessings.

Often times people jump into the camp that most fits their
personality. If you are an introvert, you'll often go about
finding a spouse by going on prayer walks alone. If you are an
extrovert, you'll probably have a new date lined up every
week. There's a balance to this dating dance. I've written about
this more in the chapter, "How to Find a Christian Spouse" if
you'd like to explore this idea in greater detail.

## Reason 6: You're Over Complicating the Process of Getting Married

One common reason many people are not married is because they are over complicating the process.

Nothing happens quickly when things get overly complicated. I'm sure we've all had experiences in life where a process becomes so complicated, you don't even want to start it. For example: I know I want to put a rain barrel next to my garage, but then I need to add gutters. But to add gutters, I need to put up new fascia. And to add new fascia, I need to tear out the old ones. And then . . . and then . . . and then . . . I think you get the point: Because it seems complicated, I am reluctant to even start.

Sometimes when we look fifty steps ahead, it hinders us from making the first step. Never is this truer than when searching for the right Christian spouse. It's a daunting task to think about finding someone to go on a date with, dating, getting more serious, engagement, planning a wedding, getting married, being married, avoiding divorce, having kids, and . . . and . . . and I think you get the point: Because it seems complicated, you are reluctant to even start.

In summary, love Jesus first, be practical, and have fun!

# Study Questions

1. Which of these reasons resonated with you? Explain.

2. There is a difference between punishment and consequences. God doesn't punish us by making us stay single, but sin does block his blessings. Do you think sin can be the cause of prolonged singleness? Why or why not? What should be done if someone feels sin is the reason they are still single?

3. For most Christians, sin is not the reason for their singleness. What should a Christian do if they want to be married but it's just not their time yet?

# Chapter 25

# 8 Expectations that Could Be Poisoning Your Dating Life

There's no shame in thinking about how you are going to meet your future spouse, what he or she will be like, or what qualities you know you want in a partner.

In fact, you can think about the future details of all this so much, you can buildup unhelpful expectations in your mind that hinder the practical side of meeting, dating, and marrying the one God has for you.

Some of you might not be ready to be so proactive. But if you feel you are ready to be more intentional in your search, here are eight of the most common unhelpful expectations that could be poisoning your chances of meeting your future spouse.

**#1: We will have the same spiritual background. Example: "I just know he will be a newer Christian like me."**

In theory, Christians typically fall into one of two categories: the "I grew up in a Christian home" category or the "I became a Christian later in life" category. When we meet someone at church for the first time, it's so easy to make a snap judgment about them after hearing when their spiritual birth date was.

Subconsciously, we typically gravitate towards people with similar backgrounds as us. If you were the pastor's daughter, you might be looking for a pastor's son. If your testimony is pretty standard, you probably have not thought about ending up with someone who was saved out of a drug addiction.

But if you only consider men and women who are "older Christians" or "younger Christians," you are drastically limiting your options. Besides, age is just a number baby. A guy whose only been saved for three years might be leaps and bounds more mature than the apathetic guy who grew up in a Christian home.

**#2: We will have the exact same theological beliefs. Example: "She will definitely love to read books by Jonathan Edwards just like me."**

There's nothing wrong with imagining how the two of you will love waking up early to pour over thick theology books written by men who have been dead for centuries.

But the reality is, your future spouse might not have the same theological flavor as you. Don't get me wrong, there are certain doctrines that all serious Christians should not bend on. But to shut down all possibilities of dating someone just because they are not reformed enough or charismatic enough will definitely cause you to miss out on meeting some really cool people.

If someone really loves Jesus, values the word of God, but doesn't fit perfectly into your theological expectations, don't feel guilty about going on a date or two to feel them out.

### #3: We will meet this certain type of way. Example: "I know we will be great friends first."

One of the most common ways to slow down your chances of finding a future spouse is by death gripping how you think the two of you will meet. Some people love the idea of marrying an awesome friend they've had since grade school. Other people feel like blind dates are the most romantic thing ever.

Odds are, you gravitate towards whatever suits your personality best. If you are a bit on the shy side, you've probably just assumed you would become friends with someone and eventually fall in love. If you are a bit more proactive by nature, your ears probably perk up when your friend talks about someone at her church she thinks would be good for you.

Don't force yourself to find your future spouse in one specific way only. Do what comes natural at first. But if it isn't working, change it up and do what's a little out of your comfort zone.

### #4: He/she will look this certain way. Example: "He must be taller than me."

Okay, this may seem a little obvious. But just because we all know we shouldn't judge people on how they look doesn't mean we don't still do it. Everyone has built in attraction triggers. You might be more attracted to girls with blond hair compared to brunettes. You might like stocky men more than skinnier guys. If you're a guy you probably want a girl shorter than you and if you're a girl you probably want a guy taller than you.

We should all marry someone we are attracted to. But first impressions can be deceiving. You'd be surprised at how attracted you can be to someone simply because they make you laugh, think you are funny, listen well, or think you make really good conversation points.

Attraction can grow the more you know someone. So get to know the person first before claiming you just aren't attracted to him or her.

**#5: We will absolutely have a [you fill in the blank] economic lifestyle. Example: "If he can't buy me a big ring, he's not the guy for me."**

While it's a huge blessing to marry someone with the same financial goals as you, assuming you will marry someone with a high paying job or a low paying job is a recipe for disaster.

Of course you should never settle for a lazy bum or a gold digger. But I promise you that if you find someone you love and who really loves you back, you'll find a happiness no money can buy.

**#6: I'll never try online dating! Example: "Me, no . . . I would never try online dating. I'm not that desperate!"**

Online dating is still relatively new. Most people looking for marriage right now did not grow up with online dating even being a possibility, thus it's a scenario most people rarely imagine. I've never talked to someone who said, "I always dreamed of meeting my spouse through an online dating website." Maybe the this will happen one day since younger generations will grow up with this option, but right now online dating is still relatively new.

If you're the type of person who tells your friends, "There's just no one to date around here," then online dating might be just right for you.

Just remember, you want God to direct your search for a spouse. There's nothing sinful about online dating or holy about traditional dating. What counts is that you are walking with God through the process. Pray about it and do what you feel God is leading you to do, even if you didn't expect to take that rout.

**#7: We will have the same hobbies and passions in life. Example: "She will definitely enjoy playing X-Box."**

"My future spouse needs to love to hike." "I need to marry a book worm like me." "I can't stand people who watch Seinfeld." "If she hates video games it's just not going to happen between us."

Okay, I get it. It's fair to want to be with someone who enjoys the same stuff as you. But just be careful you are not looking for an adventure buddy rather than a future spouse.

Hobbies come and go. Look for someone you are comfortable doing life with rather than someone who runs ultra-marathons or kayaks like you. It's a bonus if she likes that stuff, but, odds are you're going to sell that kayak once you realize you need to make room for all your kids' toys in the garage.

**#8: My social life will not need to change. Example: "He will certainly click with all my friends from college."**

There's a season for everything. While you can always value your friends from certain seasons in life, if you hold onto that season forever, you're going to miss out. When people lose common interests, often times they drift a part in their friendship. This is not bad, it's just natural.

Therefore it's not that big of a deal if your boyfriend doesn't love your best friend who lives in another state. While it would be nice if your future spouse clicked with all of your current friends, odds are it's just not going to happen. You might feel like a sellout at first, but as long as your future spouse doesn't have a problem with you still enjoying your old friends, don't limit your options by only dating people who love your friends as much as you do.

**Conclusion:**

Expectations are part of the fun. But don't poison your chances of finding a spouse by overloading your checklist. Define what's really most important to you, be open to God's leading, and think outside the box.

# Study Questions

1. What are some big expectations you have about the person you hope to marry one day? Do you think these are healthy or unhealthy to have?

2. What expectations do you hope to be able to fulfill for your future spouse? What do you hope they value in a spouse?

3. Make a list of qualities that are super important to you, moderately important to you, and not that important but would be nice if your future spouse had. If you have a close friend or someone you really trust (or a mature Bible study group), read this list to him or her and ask their opinion. Is it too narrow, not specific enough, realistic, unrealistic? Don't take one person's counsel over your own, just weigh through what they say and pray about it.

*Note: A version of this chapter first appeared as an article I wrote for RELEVANTmagazine.com.

# Chapter 26

# 3 Ways Perfectionism Can Prolong Unwanted Singleness

Not every Christian who is unmarried is unhappy about it. Some people are perfectly content with their singleness. But for the vast majority of Christians, singleness is unwanted.

A season of unwanted singleness can be extra painful for perfectionists. A perfectionist is someone who is usually extremely hands-on, likes to get things done in a specific way, and sets goals that he or she fully expects to hit right on schedule.

So if you're a perfectionist and you haven't gotten to make that engagement announcement like all your friends on social media as early as you thought, your frustration level is probably growing with every month that ticks by.

Oddly enough, perfectionism not only enhances the pain of unwanted singleness, but it can actually prolong it too. Why? Because perfectionism and romance just don't mix. So here are three ways meticulousness, precision, correctness, punctuality, and other things perfectionists love can delay your marriage from becoming a reality.

### #1: Perfectionism Causes Paralysis

Perfectionists are usually seen as go-getters. But ask any hardcore perfectionist and if she is being honest she will tell you she struggles with passivity and paralysis when a task seems too daunting to do without any errors. Perfectionism kills productivity because an extreme commitment to exactness causes an anxiety that hinders the job from just getting done.

Perfectionists hate making mistakes. Once you color outside the lines, it's darn near impossible to redeem that picture. The only thing left to do is tear that sheet out of the coloring book. But when it comes to relationships, mistakes are bit more painful. Because a perfectionist knows he can't erase a relational blemish or just tear that page out of his book, he may choose not to even start.

The truth is, real life is always messy, especially when it comes to romantic relationships. Will you make mistakes once you actively jump into the dating game? For sure. But if you are so afraid of messing up that you never actually start, the odds of finding a spouse are basically zero.

## #2: Perfectionism Hinders Realism

Lists are amazing. They make us feel organized. They give us direction on what's important. And a list can help us know when tasks are getting done. So when it comes to looking for a spouse, everyone should have some sort of list that defines what they want in a spouse.

The problem with a perfectionist is that he wants to check every little, tiny, microscopic, molecular sized requirement on that massive list. Perfectionists are usually "pass or fail" type people. You either hit all the requirements on the list or you don't fit the list. When a friend encourages a perfectionist to give a guy a chance, the response is, "But he doesn't match my list! No, I can't compromise my list!"

Checking *every* box is great when you're filing your taxes. But relationships don't work that way. Perfectionism prolongs unwanted singleness because it causes people to live in ideals rather than to be a realistic person. Idealism is the way everything "should be." And nothing slows relational progression more than the "it's not supposed to look like this" mentality.

Do you want to find a spouse? Or do you want to find a spouse in a specific way, who meets all your expectations, and fits perfectly into your world? Both options are possible, but the former is a lot more likely and the latter is nearly impossible.

### #3: Perfectionism Brings Shame

When you are committed to never making mistakes, your shame level is going to be unbearable. The Bible says humans were born with a flawed human nature (Psalm 51:5), thus through Jesus Christ we must be born again by his grace. This means that on this side of eternity, perfection is not an option. Jesus is the only guy who lived a perfect life, and he had an unfair advantage since he is the Son of God.

So perfectionism brings shame, and shame slows your unwanted singleness for a variety of reasons. Shame makes you run from dating because you think you're not good enough. Shame makes you compromise on your moral convictions because you think you need to compensate to make the opposite sex like you. And shame will cause you to date people with huge character flaws because you think that's the only type of person you can get; then you waste months or even years of dating only to finally admit you can't marry someone like that.

The perfectionist will often also heap shame onto other people. When someone makes a mistake, a perfectionist just can't let it go until he makes that person feel one inch tall. Why does a perfectionist do this? Because when it comes to negative habits, we all treat other people the way we treat ourselves. If you treat yourself harshly when you make a mistake, you will treat other people just as badly.

## Perfectionism and Relationships Don't Mix

All in all, perfectionists have some great qualities that make them super successful in certain areas of life. But most of the time a perfectionist struggles in relationships because of the messes that always happen, especially in romantic relationships.

So if you are tired of being single, perhaps shorten your list and allow for a few more flaws in yourself and others. Nothing crazy. Never turn a blind eye to someone's unrepentant sin. Don't change who you are. But if you can look past some minor details, you'll realize there are more great dating options available than you thought.

Besides, I hate to burst your bubble, but if you want to be married, you better get used to mistakes. You and your spouse will make a ton of them. A marriage will get smothered by an unrealistic need for flawlessness. So you might as well get use to the mess now if you hope to have a healthy, fun, and shame-free marriage in the future.

## Study Questions

1. How can perfectionism slow down romantic relationships from starting? How can perfectionism hinder romantic relationships from flourishing once a relationship has begun?

2. What's the problem with demanding perfection from others? What's the problem with demanding it from yourself? Do you think how we treat ourselves is similar to how we treat other people?

3. People get mad, people breakup and then get back together, and "I'm sorry" moments seem to be needed far more than we would like. Why are relationships so messy? How can you prepare now in your singleness to handle the messiness once you do get into a relationship (or get married)?

*Note: A version of this chapter first appeared as an article I wrote for RELEVANTmagazine.com.

# Chapter 27:

# 7 Points to Consider About Online Dating (and dating in general)

Many Christians struggle with the idea of online dating. They wonder, "How does God feel about online dating? Does he see it as not trusting him? Is online dating a sin?"

While the Bible obviously never directly talks about online dating, the wisdom found in Scripture can certainly help us answer many of the common questions Christian singles have when they are considering online dating.

So here are 7 points to consider when it comes to online dating as a Christian single.

### #1: It's Not About How You Meet. It's About Who You Date and Then Marry

God isn't concerned with how you go about meeting a prospective spouse (as long as it is not unwise or sinful). What he really cares about is who you decide to spend time with, date, and then marry.

We should use wisdom here. It would be a lack of solid reasoning to assume you have a good chance of meeting a great Christian spouse by bar-hopping every weekend. Likewise, randomly throwing your profile online for the whole world to see is probably not going to be an effective way of finding a godly spouse with a desire to glorify God. So in that sense, God really does care how you go about trying to meet people.

But as long as you are relying on biblical wisdom, listening to the counsel of your Christian community, and truly trying to honor God, there is nothing inherently sinful about online dating. Again, what God really cares about is who you marry, not how you meet this person.

God commands Christians to marry other Christians (1 Corinthians 7:39, 2 Corinthians 6:14). As long as this is your goal, there is nothing wrong with using online dating.

## #2: Don't Use Online Dating If You Lack Discretion

While online dating is not a sin, there are many dangers to online dating for Christian singles. Social media is so tempting to misuse because it is so easy to portray ourselves however we want. We can take the perfect picture, phrase our sentences just right, and reveal only the most flattering information about ourselves.

So if you decide to give online dating a chance, you have to know yourself. Are you easily wowed and gullible? Do you really think everyone online is there with good intentions?

If you know you have a history of picking guys who are handsome rather than honoring, rich rather than respectful, or charismatic rather than Christ-centered, then you need to be very careful with online dating. If you are a guy who instantly maxes out the credit cards when a pretty girl gives you attention, again, you need to be extra cautious when mingling online.

Be honest. If you lack discretion, if you are not known for your discernment, or if you are easily wowed by surface information, then online dating might not be for you. If nothing else, at least ask a friend to keep you accountable as you search for a godly spouse online.

## #3: Be Transparent With Someone You Trust When Trying Online Dating

Online dating is a pretty bold move. You are making a serious step forward in being very active and not passive in your hopes to find a spouse. The danger here is that once you start pressing forward, you might press forward too hard and compromise since you want to find a Christian spouse so bad.

This is where Christian accountability will really benefit you. Don't be a closet online dater. You don't have to broadcast it to the world. I know online dating might be embarrassing for some (even though it shouldn't be). But make sure you include other Christians in this process who you respect. Bounce ideas off of them. Let them do some profile searching too on your behalf.

Also, including others in the process of online dating is just a good safety tip. If you are going to meet someone you met online for the first time, it's not a bad idea to bring a friend along. If the person you are dating is solid, he (or she) will respect your concern for safety and appreciate the effort you are putting forth to find a solid spouse. At minimum, tell other people who you are going to meet and where you are meeting him or her.

## #4: Be Serious in Your Search, But Don't Take Each Date Too Seriously

Dating is an emotional rollercoaster. It's unavoidable. So I'm not going to sit here and tell you not to get emotional. I know that is impossible to do perfectly. And quite frankly, this is a serious thing. Trying to find the person you are going to spend the rest of your life with is no small matter.

With all that said, you are going to wear yourself out if you take each date too seriously. Do your best to keep calm, have fun, and don't over think it. Just go on a date and enjoy it for what it is . . . a date.

Will you probably jump way ahead in your mind, imagining if this person will make a good dad to your 3 children named Heather, Austin, and Frank? Probably. But then come back to reality and live with realistic expectations. You are probably not going to meet your future husband or wife on the first date or two you go on when you begin online dating.

Try to enjoy each date for what it is. It's okay if you don't go on another date with that person. It's all a part of the process.

### #5: Don't View Each Date as Pass or Fail

I believe the intention behind dating should be to find a spouse. If you are dating people just to have fun or fill some emotional need in yourself, that's not healthy and will definitely lead you into sin. There's enough temptation to overcome in your life. So you don't need to become emotionally or physically involved with someone you know you are not going to marry.

There are still beneficial parts, however, to dating even if that specific relationship does not result in marriage. Don't date people you know you won't marry. But also know you are probably not going to marry the first, second, or third person you date.

Dating people enhances your character. It increases your discernment. It refines what qualities you really care about in another person. Dating people will force you to realize things about yourself you would otherwise never have learned. It can prepare you to become the person you need to be to thrive when you finally do meet your future spouse. If done right, the dating process (including online dating) should enhance your ability to walk with God and follow his leading.

So don't view each dating relationship as pass or fail depending on if you marry that person or not. Learn what God wants you to learn through each date.

### #6: Don't Forget the True Goal of Dating/Online Dating

The most important goal of dating is to figure out if this person is your future spouse. If the relationship ends, you accomplished the goal of dating because you've learned this person is not the one for you. It might seem like a waste of time if you dated someone and then broke up; but if through dating this person you learned he or she is not your future spouse, then you did not waste your time.

Wasting your time in dating only happens when you continue to date someone even after you know for certain you are not going to marry him or her. How long should you date someone? You should date them as long as you need to help you know for certain that God wants you to marry him or her. For some this is a few months. For others this is a few years.

I believe each relationship really is different. But if I had to put a number on it, I personally think a healthy dating season is around a year or two. You want to give yourself enough time to really get to know this person. But you also don't want to wait too long since the temptation will be to act like your married when you're not (emotionally, sexually, financially, and etcetera).

You'll have to walk with God on deciding how long you should date someone before you marry him or her. Just remember the true goal of dating, which is to decide whether this person is the one you want to marry or not. Once you've decided that, the dating relationship eventually needs to end either through breaking up or through getting engaged.

## #7: Use Online Dating When Traditional Dating Is Not Working

I think traditional dating should be your first option. It's more ideal to sit down with a real person and get to know someone. It's just more practical to become friends with someone through common interests, environments, or community groups. But if these traditional means are not working, it might be time to give online dating a chance.

For example, if you are nineteen and want to be married, I don't think there is anything wrong with that. I know plenty of nineteen-year-olds who are mature enough to get married. Will they have trouble? Yeah, but everyone has trouble in marriage. Trouble can happen at any age. But I digress. My point is that if you are nineteen, you probably don't need to online date. You have time.

However, if for example you have entered your thirties or forties and you haven't been on a date in years but you want to be married, it's time to try something different. If you don't feel God is leading you to online date, then don't. But you need to be realistic. The older you get, the less options you will have. If you are a bit older but still have plenty of great dating options because of your church, your community, or your very "thoughtful" friends, then you probably don't need to online date.

In short, if what you've been doing is not working and you want to find a Christian spouse, give online dating a chance. I can't promise you it will work. But at least you won't have to wonder if you've done all you can do.

Online dating is not a sin. God doesn't feel negatively about online dating. The Bible does not condemn unorthodox dating because it doesn't really talk about dating. The Bible tells us what we need to know, and what we need to know is that God wants Christians to marry other Christians. Besides that, it really doesn't matter too much how you meet.

God is still sovereign over your relational life no matter what course you take to meet your spouse. Even if you try online dating, it's not like you need to trust God any less than you would if you were trying traditional dating.

Walk with God, be biblically grounded, and stay focused on the real goals of dating. Put Christ first. If you do these things, online dating might really benefit you.

# Study Questions

1. Do you think you are at a point in life where online dating is a good option? Why or why not?

2. What do you think the goal of dating should be?

3. Are you a person with good discernment? How can you guard against assuming the best of people who may have bad intentions when it comes to traditional dating and online dating?

# Chapter 28

# Why You Should Stop "Putting God First to Find a Spouse"

What I'm about to say is going to come off as blasphemous at first. So please read this whole chapter to get the full context of this statement. If you do, I believe you will better enjoy your Christian singleness and be better situated to find a Christian spouse. Alright, here it goes:

Stop trying to put God first as a way of finding your future spouse.

See? I told you that was going to be irritating. What am I saying? Notice the last part of this sentence, "as a way of finding your future spouse." Every Christian must always put God first. But I would argue that if you are "putting God first" as a means to something other than God, you are not actually putting God first.

Where your treasure is, there your heart will be also (Matthew 6:21). In other words, whatever is your end goal is what you are truly putting first. Seeking God first to find a spouse is really seeking a spouse first.

### God Cannot Be Mocked, So It's Pointless to "Put God First to Find a Spouse"

As Christians, we believe God is in control. Therefore when we want to be married but we have not found a spouse yet, it's easy to assume God is mad at us. If God is in control and he has not blessed me with a spouse, he must be angry with me, right? Am I being punished for my past sins? Is that why God has not blessed me with a spouse?

As a result of this thinking, we assume the solution is to please God to increase our chances of being blessed with what we want. It's kind of like Santa, "He's making a list, and checking it twice, he's going find out who's been naughty or nice." This is not how God works.

Since God does indeed want us to put God first, and the Bible does seem to indicate that when you please God he will bless you (Matthew 6:33), it's logical to assume that if you want God to bless you with a Christian spouse, all you have to do is put God first.

While there are fragments of truth here, this thinking is definitely not totally biblical. Just because you don't have what you want does not mean God is mad at you. Likewise, just because you have all the earthly blessings you do want does not mean God is pleased with you. Earthly blessings are not the thermometer of God's pleasure in us. That type of thinking is rooted in "prosperity gospel" theology.

God's ultimate gifts always come in the form of himself. When God is pleased with you, you will have a deeper relationship with God. When God is pleased with you, your joy in God will abound. What God wants most of all is to be first in every area of our lives. He wants this for himself and for us. When God is first, he is glorified and we are blessed by his presence.

So when we try to put God first as a way of attaining some other blessing, like a Christian spouse, God sees right through this.

"Do not be deceived: God is not mocked, for whatever one sows, that will he also reap. For the one who sows to his own flesh will from the flesh reap corruption, but the one who sows to the Spirit will from the Spirit reap eternal life. (Galatians 6:7-8)

We reap what we sow. When we seek to please God, we reap a reward in God.

### "Putting God First to Find a Spouse" Is Biblically Backwards

Seeking God first is not a means to end (like finding a spouse). Seeking God first is an end in itself. The point of life is God.

I know pastors mean well when they say we need to put God first, then our marriage, then our kids, then our friends, then our jobs, and etc. But a more biblical way to put it would be to say that we should put God first in our marriage, in our parenting, in our friendships, in our pursuit of a spouse, and etc.

God is not just the most important category. God should overwhelm all categories of life. God doesn't want to be placed in one box, even if it's our first and most important box. Putting God first in everything is the goal, not just above everything.

So in the context of finding a spouse, you'll have to work on the motivation of your heart if you hope to avoid trying to manipulate God, which never works anyways.

Therefore, rather than putting God first "to find a Christian spouse," you should seek to put God first "in" your search for a Christian spouse. Seek God first and use your search for a spouse as a way to glorify God. Don't use glorifying God as a way to find a spouse. To seek God first to find a Christian spouse would be like marrying a woman for her money, "If I love you will you give me your money?" In this scenario, the man loves what the woman can give him, not the woman herself. The same is true when we try to love God with the motivation of getting a Christian spouse. We are not really loving God. We are just seeking him so he will give us what we want.

The true blessing of a Christian marriage is that it helps you glorify, serve, and love God better (unless you have the gift of singleness). If you're asking God for a spouse and your motivation is not rooted in pleasing God, then you're asking God for a secondary gift. God wants to give you the best. So he often waits to bless us with a spouse until we are ready to use our marriage in service to him rather than using God to serve our future marriage.

Honestly, one of the scariest things is when God finally gives you a Christian spouse even though you want him or her for all the wrong reasons. God will use the pain of this marriage, rather than the joy of a healthy marriage, to draw you to himself and help you put him first.

**Odds Are, God Wants You To Be Married. So Put God First and Go For It!**

I think one of the reasons the advice to "Put God first to find a Christian spouse" has resonated with so many Christian singles is because many view these two desires as opposing one another.

It's as though if Christians were to admit they really did want a Christian spouse, it might compromise their other desire to put

God first. The problem here is that you view having a Christian spouse as a different desire than pleasing God. These two desires should be the same. You should want a Christian spouse to assist your desire to please God.

These two desires never have to oppose one another. Marriage is a blessing from God (just as singleness is). You never have to feel ashamed for having a desire to be married (or single). You can glorify God in your search for a spouse by doing it the right way, for the right reasons, and right alongside God as he leads and directs you.

Having said all that, if you know the desire to find a Christian spouse has become an idol to you, which means it has usurped rather than supported your desire to love God, then you shouldn't go for it right away.

Repent of making a Christian spouse an idol. Take a break from pursuing a spouse. And once you feel you can seek a spouse with the intent of pleasing God, then go for it. The desire for a Christian spouse only opposes our desire to please God when we want a spouse more than God. But when we want God, and we want a Christian spouse to help us in our service to God, God is happy with this desire. Don't be ashamed of it. Put God first and go for it!

As I've said throughout this book, there are definitely Christians who are called to a life of singleness. But the vast majority are called to marriage. Either way, every one of us is called to glorify God in all that we do. Therefore, for those of you who want to find a Christian spouse, ask yourself "Why?" Is it for selfish reasons? Or is it for God-honoring reasons? Repent of the former and pursue the latter.

When the glory of God is as the root of our desire to be married, our desire to be married pleases God. Use everything, including your search for a spouse, as a way to glorify God. Don't try to glorify God so you can get a Christian spouse. Try to get a Christian spouse as another way of glorifying God.

## Study Questions

1. Have you ever tried to "Put God first to find a Christian spouse?" Do you think there is anything wrong with putting God first in order to be blessed with something else that you want? Why or why not?

2. What should be the motive behind wanting to be married?

3. What's the difference between "putting God above everything else" compared to "putting God first in everything"? Is God supposed to be in his own category that we put first in life or is he supposed to be first in every category that we have in life? Explain what you think about all this.

# Chapter 29

# Love Is Always Dangerous . . . Love Anyway

*The LORD God took the man and put him in the Garden of Eden to work it and take care of it. And the LORD God commanded the man, "You are free to eat from any tree in the garden; but you must not eat from the tree of the knowledge of good and evil, for when you eat from it you will certainly die."-*
*Genesis 2:15-17*

Love is dangerous. It comes with so much potential for pain because true love must involve real choice. The definition of risk is to "expose (someone or something valued) to danger, harm, or loss." This sounds a lot like real love.

To avoid all danger, harm, or loss (i.e. risk) God would have had to remove all choice, all risk of people not loving him; but in the process of doing this he would also erase any scenario of true love taking place.

God will have none of this "safe love" because he knows this is an impossibility. Rather than relational safety, God chose love, for he knew he could not have both. Because of his commitment to choose love no matter the consequence, he gave the summons that "You are free . . ." (Genesis 2:16). As his mallet hit like a judge's final rule in the courtroom, his decree was made, man was free to choose good or evil, and there was no going back, by his choice, because of his love.

With our freedom came not the possibility of our rebellion, but the guarantee of it. God knew that if he was going to have a people who could choose to share in his love, he was also going to have a people who could choose against it. He placed the tree of the knowledge of good and evil in the middle of the garden not wondering if we will eat it, but knowing we would, "for when you eat from it you will certainly die" (Genesis 2:17). He says "when" not "if" we eat this fruit.

The staggering fact is that God chose to love anyway. He knew we would choose against his love, he knew how people would hurt themselves with their free choice to not love God, but, nevertheless, he went forward with the plan.

Risk is only worth taking when the possibility of reward is that much greater. The consequences of rebelling against God cannot be fathomed by the human mind. Eternal punishment is a thought too big and too awful to really grasp. But for God to risk all that pain to himself and to people, we are forced to ask the question: How great must his love be?

For God to make us anyway, to risk all that pain so there would be a chance for true eternal love for some of us to enjoy forever, shows that although we cannot comprehend the punishment of being separated from his love, we certainly then will not be able to comprehend how incredible this eternal union with him in love will be, as he truly is the God of love "able to do far more abundantly than all that we ask or think" (Ephesians 3:20).

God knew we would eat the fruit, but he made us anyway. God loved anyway. Being made in his image, we too must love anyway if we are to love at all. There is no safe love out there. There is no romance without risk, no relationship without remorse, no true friendships without fears coming true. Choice is essential to true love, therefore danger will always be there too. But like God, we must remember that although pain is really a matter of "when" and not "if," love really is worth the risk.

I don't know what path God has for you. I don't know who you are going to meet, marry, not meet, or not marry. I just know that when you love, it will be amazing. But it will hurt too. If we hope to love like God, we must learn to love anyway.

## Study Questions

1. Does opening yourself up to truly love someone and be loved by someone scare you at all? Do you ever think about the pain that can come along with real love? How has this shaped your decisions to love others or not love others?

2. Why is love so risky? Why is there always potential for pain?

3. Despite all the pain that will come into our lives when we choose to love other people, especially when it comes to loving someone in a monogamous relationship, why should we love anyway?

# Conclusion

# When the Answers Don't Come

# Chapter 30

# God's Love Is Enough

Despite my best efforts to answer the many common questions Christian singles have, I know this book will come woefully short. Life just presents too many questions and unknowns for one book to give advice about all the possible scenarios singles will encounter.

So my last piece of advice revolves around what to do when you can't figure out what to do. When you've done the research, read your Bible, prayed about it, asked other mature Christians, and you still are confused about your life and what God is up to – what do you do then?

### God's Love Is Great Enough to Outweigh Life's Confusions

The questions that stem from singleness and relationships (and all the other questions about life in general) can be a weight on our shoulders, replacing our joy for life with worry and confusion. I was recently feeling burdened about something specific in my own life, so I began to pray. Sometimes God gives me specific direction that helps with my current problem. But this time he didn't. I felt like he simply said, "I love you."

Immediately life made sense again.

Sometimes all we need to hear is that God loves us. It may sound cliché, but simply knowing that you are loved by God makes life worth living, no matter how difficult the present situation.

Likewise, no matter how favorable the situation, life is pure drudgery when we don't know that we are loved, especially when we don't know we are loved by God. We were made to live off of the love of God. We weren't made to be filled by our careers, family life, relationships, and all the other things that we fill our time with.

We were made to be fueled by God.

### God's Love Is More Than Enough to Conquer Your Fears in Life

Complicated problems don't always require complicated solutions. What we need the most in life is to know that God loves us.

> "Do not set your heart on what you will eat or drink; do not worry about it. For the pagan world runs after such things, and your Father knows that you need them. But seek his kingdom, and these things will be given to you as well. Do not be afraid, little flock, for your Father has been pleased to give you the kingdom" (Luke 12:29-32).

I wonder how much better life would be if we simply held tightly to the reality of God's love for us? So whatever the issue, dwell upon God's love for you.

> "See how very much our Father loves us, for he calls us his children, and that is what we are!" (1 John 3:1).

When you know deep down in the recesses of your soul that God loves you and cares for you, your feelings of anxiety are changed. Your circumstances may be the same. Your unwanted singleness might still linger. And your knowledge on what to do next may still be lacking. But your peace will be perfect when you know that God loves you. God's love is enough.

> "Give all your worries and cares to God, for he cares about you." (1 Peter 5:7, NLT)

## Even When You Don't Have Answers to Life's Confusing Questions, God's Love Is Enough

When you know that God loves you, life just makes sense. And even when it doesn't, you're okay with it, because you know you are loved deeply by God. The lens of love clarifies the confusion of life. Let us continually seek to live life through this lens and no other.

So if you're going through a rough time in life, don't immediately try and solve the external problem. Get to the root of the matter, which is that your circumstances are causing you to doubt God's love for you, and thus you feel anxious. Dwell on the reality that God loves you with an everlasting love (Jeremiah 31:3), and see if this does not change everything.

God often does give us answers to the many questions we have. I hope this book has helped answer a few in regards to Christian singleness. But ultimately God's love is always the answer we need the most.

# Study Questions

1. Why is it so important to know that God truly loves you immensely? How will we feel when we don't know this?

2. What are some practical ways you can be reminded of God's love for you?

3. What have you learned from this study? Perhaps finish this study by writing out a prayer, asking God to help you live what you've learned. Ask him to guide you through your singleness. And ask him to help you glorify him in every season you will experience in life now and in the future.

# Thank You

Dear readers,

I want to thank you for giving me the privilege to walk with you through this amazing season of singleness. It's not an easy season, but as we both know, God desires this to be a fruitful time for your relationship with him.

I hope you've benefited from the many topics we've covered here. My prayer is that God will use this book to bring love, security, and guidance to all who read it.

Lastly, I have a favor to ask. Would you take two or three minutes and write a review of this book on Amazon? The reason I ask is because one of the best ways for other people to find this book is for those who have read it to write a review. Amazon gives more attention to books with reviews and people are more likely to read something when others have already tried it and liked it.

You can just go to the Amazon website and type in "The Ultimate Guide to Christian Singleness," click the book cover, and then you should be on the correct page to write a short review. Thank you!

Please stay in touch with me by visiting my website at ApplyGodsWord.com. This is the central hub for all my content. All my social media channels can be found there as well. We are on Facebook, Twitter, and YouTube, so you can head to those platforms and just type in "ApplyGodsWord.com" to find us.

And if you have any questions or comments, you can always email me at MarkBallenger@ApplyGodsWord.com.

I hope nothing but the best for you!

For God's glory and our good, all through the power of Christ,

-Mark

Made in the USA
Thornton, CO
02/25/23 18:14:48